HOW TO PROTECT YOUR MONEY OFFSHORE

P9-EEA-006

Arnold S. Goldstein, J.D., LL.M., Ph.D.

GARRETT PUBLISHING, INC.

HOW TO PROTECT YOUR MONEY OFFSHORE
By Arnold S. Goldstein, J.D., LL.M., Ph.D.
Copyright 1996 by Garrett Publishing, Inc.

Published by Garrett Publishing, Inc.
384 S. Military Trail
Deerfield Beach, FL 33442
954-480-8543 (Phone)
954-698-0057 (Fax)

This publication is designed to provide accurate and authoritative information in regard to the subject matter covered. It is sold with the understanding that neither the publisher nor the author is engaged in rendering the legal, accounting, or other professional service. If legal advice or other expert assistance is required, the services of a competent professional should be sought. *From A Declaration of Principals jointly adopted by the Committee of the American Bar Association and a Committee of Publishers.*

WEALTHSAVERS® is a registered trademark of Garrett Publishing, Inc.

Library of Congress Cataloging-in-publication Data

Goldstein, Arnold S.
  How to Protect Your Money Offshore
  p.   cm.
  Includes bibliographical references.
  ISBN   1-880539-41-1
  1. Asset protection. 2. Banks and banking, International.
3. Banks and banking, foreign. 4. Banks and banking — United States. 5. Privacy. 6. Tax Havens.
I. Title

Printed in the United States of America
10 9 8 7 6 5 4 3 2 1

"It's not difficult to make money today...

the trick is to keep it!"

MEET AMERICA'S
#1 WEALTHSAVER

You have undoubtedly heard of Dr. Arnold S. Goldstein.

He has done it! Not once, but for tens of thousands of far-sighted Americans demanding rock-solid financial protection — people from every background and corner of the world who have finally found true security for themselves and their families following the very same wealth preservation strategies you will read about in this book.

You have seen or heard him discuss his powerful financial protection strategies on countless radio and TV talk shows (including CNN, CNBC and NBC's Today Show) or before one of the many groups that welcome him as a featured seminar and meeting speaker.

You possibly read about him and his wealth-preservation concepts in one of the numerous business and finance magazines... *Inc... Fortune... Money... CFO... Entrepreneur... Success... Venture... Business Week... Bottom Line...* to name a few.

You may be one of the hundreds of thousands of concerned people who found new financial security in the pages of his best-selling *Offshore Havens* or *Asset Protection Secrets*, or one of over 100 other books or 300-plus articles on wealth protection.

A veteran lawyer, who has practiced asset protection law for over 30 years; his tactics are fully battle-tested. He is now the managing partner in the firm of Arnold S. Goldstein & Associates. He is a member of the Massachusetts and federal bars.

A scholar's scholar, he holds five academic degrees from leading universities (including graduate law degrees in taxation, an MBA and a Ph.D. in economic and business policy from Northeastern University where he is professor *emeritus*). He has also taught law at several other universities and was a postdoctoral research scholar on offshore trusts on the faculty of law at the London School of Economics.

He is a member of the Offshore Institute, the Oxford Club and numerous other organizations devoted to financial protection and is now considered one of America's leading experts on the formation and use of offshore asset protection trusts as well as other international and domestic strategies to conserve wealth. He enjoys hearing from his many readers and can be reached at (954) 420-4990.

TABLE OF CONTENTS

WHY YOU MUST READ THIS BOOK TODAY!

"Life," *John F. Kennedy once said, "isn't always fair. Even the venal can get rich."*

"And the virtuous can as easily get poor," I would add.

That reality hit my old Army pal Charlie smack between the eyes when the IRS demanded he shell out $475,000. Because Charlie was a part-owner of a business that folded several years earlier, he was personally liable for its unpaid withholding taxes. His partner? Dead and buried. Poor Charlie knew absolutely nothing about the firm's finances but was left holding the bag.

Within three months Charlie had lost everything... his savings... expensive home... two cars... a vacation condo... even his pension. At 52, Charlie had nothing left but his family and faithful retriever, Sam.

The IRS blitz financially and emotionally devastated Charlie and his wife Martha. Charlie's still too depressed to work, but he and Martha scrimp by on Martha's pittance salary as a supermarket cashier. Charlie's two kids quit college. With nothing to fall back on, Charlie and Martha are one step away from welfare.

It's mighty tough to think you're financially secure only to be suddenly wiped out. Ask Charlie!

Charlie's hardly the only casualty I came across lately. My next door neighbor recently lost his business and creditors seized his $300,000 home. His nest egg is gone forever! My stockbroker? His wife abandoned *him* but not his $140,000 in cash and securities that she walked away with. My own ex-secretary is now elderly and her husband's nursing home bills will consume their every last dime. So much for financial security!

Two of my golfing pals are really sweating. As directors of a large corporation they're fighting $20 million lawsuits that several stockholders filed against them. With no insurance and a lifetime accumulation of assets, Henry and Ben have plenty to lose. I bet you know your share of people in the same fix.

Big lawsuits. Business failure. Tax troubles. Divorce. Catastrophic illness.

The list is endless. The point is that you also can feel safe and secure today and be as suddenly wiped out tomorrow. You are now vulnerable and will remain vulnerable *unless* you protect yourself. Financial disaster can destroy your future *unless* you act now to shelter what you own. There's no way to avoid it. Today there are just *too* many ways to get into financial trouble . That is how it is in America in the 1990s, and it will get worse in the years ahead.

There are loads of people like Charlie... people oblivious to the reality that they too *can* be financially sideswiped when they least expect it.

These are people — probably people very much like yourself — who only know how to make money in their own business or profession but have absolutely no idea how to protect their wealth. But protecting wealth is what I *do* know and what I will reveal to you in this book. I want you to see how a revolutionary new asset protection and wealth-preservation system can give you the solid financial security in these unsafe times that it has provided so many other farsighted Americans.

NOT ONLY FOR THE RICH AND POWERFUL

At first glance, you probably thought this was a book only for the rich and powerful. If so, you're dead wrong. The rich and powerful *already* have their wealth sheltered by some of America's best legal minds. I know. Some of America's wealthiest families are clients of mine, and I have helped them and their families obtain lifelong financial security following precisely the wealth preservation strategy I will now reveal to you.

But my typical asset-protection clients are neither rich nor famous. They are everyday folks — doctors, plumbers, retailers, developers — mainstream Americans from a thousand different occupations who get up each morning to do a day's work. Their only goal is to build a nest egg and keep it secure.

Whoever they are, whatever their backgrounds, however great or small their wealth, most believe our society has gone amuck. They no longer believe our legal system will protect their wealth. They no longer trust a government hell-bent on confiscating, taxing or misappropriating their wealth. They no longer trust their neighbors, friends, business associates, employees, or even their own families. All are seen as potential litigants. They know that no matter how careful or disciplined or honest you may be, financial security and freedom can never truly be achieved because one poor decision — or simply being in the wrong place at the wrong time — can cost you everything you have worked years to build. This is how it is whether you have $10,000 or $10 million to lose! If you agree with this message, then keep reading.

CIRCLE THE WAGONS

Like myself and so many others, you may not like the world as it has become. But you cannot change it. All you can do is protect yourself so that you can survive in the world as it is.

To survive you will need your very own financial self-defense plan, a plan that can protect:

- *everything you own*

- *against any financial or legal threat*

- *under all circumstances*

You cannot afford to settle for less. But the probability is that you now have absolutely no wealth protection plan and certainly not the solid financial defense plan I describe. If your wealth is still exposed and vulnerable, you are not alone. *Nine out of ten American families with a net worth over $500,000 have absolutely no financial protection!* These are the optimists. These are the procrastinators. These are people who will someday learn a very bitter lesson.

And I know how bitter a lesson it can be. Frankly, I've seen too many grown men cry, too many marriages collapse and too many good people destroyed by a legal or financial catastrophe. The tragedy in nearly every case is that their financial losses could easily have been avoided. Unfortunately, these folks just didn't protect themselves, nor realize they *needed* protection!

That's why I wrote this book. I want to show you a *new* and superior way to safeguard your assets against *any* financial threat. My commitment is to help you and your family enjoy the same lifetime financial security that so many of my clients now enjoy. This is no pipe dream. You can legally and effectively protect your assets against *every* danger and *every* threat.

How to Protect Your Money Offshore reveals this proven strategy that can protect you as it has thousands of other individuals from every walk of life who wanted *their* wealth sheltered against financial crisis. The strategy I detail in this book was their blueprint to an impenetrable financial fortress against lawsuits... creditors... bankruptcy... the IRS... divorce... probate... nursing-home costs... and so many other wealth-destroyers that we must all vigorously guard against, no matter who we are.

You'll find this book vital to your future whether or not you now have a financial protection plan. If your assets are presently unprotected, you'll discover how to build your financial fortress from scratch. If you *think* your assets *are* now well protected, you may find a far more powerful wealth-saving strategy. Either way, you have in your hands your key to the financially secure future that we all want but so few of us achieve.

JOIN THE UNTOUCHABLES

Of course, there are many legal strategies that one can use to protect wealth. With 30 years in the trenches as an asset protection lawyer, I have used *each and every* one to protect my clients' assets, and I invented a few more of my own. My best-selling *Asset Protection Secrets* reveals over 300 proven ways to protect assets with the familiar domestic trusts, limited partnerships, corporations, co-tenancies, state exemptions and the many other wealth-preservation tactics.

The problem is that most of these asset-protection strategies are like hunting elephants with a BB gun. When a sue-happy lawyer comes after you or Uncle Sam eyeballs your bank account, you need even *stronger* protection. *But how do you get that fortress solid protection?* The answer is within these pages!

For financial protection you must also do more than simply shelter your assets from those who *want* them. You must also privatize your wealth and keep a low profile. But you know how impossible that is in a cyber-tech age that makes your financial life an open book. *So how do you gain real privacy for your financial affairs?* The answer is within these pages!

Financial security also requires financial growth. You must *keep more*, not less of what you earn. Do you think that will happen in the years ahead? I don't think so. The government is your pocketbook's most menacing enemy. Despite all the political rhetoric, Uncle Sam will abscond with *more and more* of your wealth. What he won't grab through taxes, he will confiscate or seize under another pretense. *So, how will you protect your wealth from Uncle Sam?* The answer is within these pages!

And we cannot talk intelligently about wealth protection without examining what is happening right now to your savings, investments, or even your pension. Perhaps you haven't noticed that you have much *less* spending power now than you did only a decade ago. You can expect even *less* spending power next year. Yes, our inflation appears in check and our stock market is up, but don't fool yourself. It's the quiet before the storm. Our economy is a house of cards. Behind the facade our government is rigging a massive economic re-engineering scheme that threatens every last dollar you saved. What's worse, Washington will hold your money hostage right here in America where it can leisurely be plucked clean. *Don't you think your wealth would be better protected elsewhere?* The answer is within these pages!

Whether or not you have found it difficult to make money in America, I tell you that you will find it impossible to *keep* it in America. What was once the land of financial opportunity is now overrun by hordes of avaricious lawyers and litigants and armies of faceless bureaucrats who share one unmistakable objective: to grab *your* wealth!

You need no shocking stories, statistics and revelations to prove the point. Simply open your eyes.

REGAINING YOUR FINANCIAL FREEDOM

My many years as an asset protection and wealth preservation lawyer taught me one critical lesson! **The only *safe* way to hold wealth today is in an offshore asset protection trust.** This special trust is the only way to adequately guard against the inevitable attacks on your financial freedom and security.

I have established offshore asset protection trusts for hundreds of very grateful clients. None has lost even one thin dime of trust assets to *any* financial threat. Moreover, these now-financially secure people enjoy *greater* privacy and more profitable investments than even before.

That's why I call the offshore asset protection trust the WealthSaver® Trust. In fact, I registered the name WealthSaver as my own trademark because it so aptly describes what this unique trust *can* do for you. My WealthSaver Trust is a greatly improved version of the standard offshore asset protection trust because it protects wealth even *more* effectively. My goal is to make the WealthSaver Trust the #1 *financial protection tool in America today*. Already it has won acclaim from leading lawyers and financial experts both here in America and in other countries.

This book will tell you everything you *must* know about the WealthSaver Trust. I will show you *how* it works and *why* it works. I will thoroughly explain and detail how it can so superbly protect your own wealth from:

- lawsuits, creditors, the IRS, ex-spouses and other legal predators.

- snoops who are anxious to eyeball your wealth and financial affairs.

- confiscatory taxes.

- a sagging U.S. economy and certain wealth erosion.

- and much more.

You will not find this another half-baked wealth protection scheme. The fact is that only the WealthSaver Trust can provide total protection to those who are truly serious about preserving and conserving their wealth.

Of course, I anticipate questions and skepticism.

You will ask whether protecting your money offshore is *safe*. Rest assured, your money will be far safer offshore than it is here in America.

You will ask whether it is legal. Rest assured, the WealthSaver program is 100-percent legitimate.

You will ask whether it works. For that answer, I invite you to ask a few of the tens of thousands of Americans who now have nearly $3 trillion secured in their own offshore trusts. I leave it to *them* to make *my* case!

The WealthSaver Trust is truly the perfect financial protection weapon for our times. It is to wealth preservation what the living trust is to probate avoidance. But all new ideas and concepts meet resistance and skepticism. For most people who need the WealthSaver Trust, the obstacle will always be *ignorance* and *fear.*

You also may have been programmed to believe that offshore finance is only for crooks, frauds or the super-rich. Your own financial planner, lawyer and accountant will probably advise you to forget about it. They will tell you it's "too risky, too expensive, too bothersome." Odds are *they* don't know one thing more about offshore trusts than you do. But *you* will know considerably more about them once you read this book.

So, this book's mission is to substitute information and facts for ignorance and fear. I formed hundreds of WealthSaver Trusts, and I work closely with leading lawyers and other financial professionals throughout the country who have established thousands more. I have championed the WealthSaver Trust on hundreds of radio and TV talk shows (including CNN, CNBC and the NBC's Today Show). I conducted countless WealthSaver Trust seminars and gave people the opportunity to hear about The WealthSaver Trust at many more professional and business meetings. As a research scholar on the law faculty of the London School of Economics, I thoroughly researched the offshore trust with some of the finest minds in international law and finance — and I designed it to work even more effectively for Americans. My results have been published in numerous books and professional journals.

The offshore trust is gradually gaining recognition. And it will continue to do so as financial professionals seek better ways to protect their clients' wealth. But learning takes time and most Americans don't have time. They need protection *right now*!

WHAT YOU WILL FIND IN THIS BOOK

You probably know absolutely nothing about offshore trusts, or what I call the WealthSaver Trust. Only one in ten Americans do. So I start at ground zero.

Chapter One will give you a basic overview of the WealthSaver Trust. You will see how the trust is organized and generally functions. This overview provides the framework for later chapters.

Chapters Two through Five each highlights one of the four big benefits you can gain from establishing your own WealthSaver Trust — asset protection, privacy, global investing and tax and estate planning advantages.

Chapter Six overviews the more popular WealthSaver Trust havens and explains how to select the financial center that can best protect your wealth.

Chapter Seven, the final chapter, is perhaps the most important: It will answer your many questions on how you can easily and economically start your very own WealthSaver program.

I use a Q&A format because it's the easiest way to digest complex subjects. I am asked these same important questions time and again from clients and seminar attendees, and so I can accurately predict your questions concerning the WealthSaver Trust. Please call me if I overlooked or failed to adequately answer an important question. I would be delighted to chat because I enjoy helping people gain the financial freedom they need and deserve!

This is a book for ordinary people who can benefit from the WealthSaver Trust. It is not a technical text for professionals, although many lawyers, accountants and other financial professionals can undoubtedly profit from it. As such, *How to Protect Your Money Offshore* can only speak in generalities. It is not intended to be a substitute for professional advice.

While a great deal of care has been taken to insure accurate and current information, the ideas, general principles and recommendations in this book are subject to complex and ever-changing laws, regulations and court rulings. You are urged to consult an appropriate professional before you act on any of the recommendations or comments made in this book. We cannot accept any responsibility for any loss that may otherwise arise.

How to Protect Your Money Offshore can, however, be your passport to financial freedom once you understand the many ways this special trust can benefit you. If it only encourages you to learn more it will have done its job. So I encourage you to seek other points of view by reading other good books and journal articles on the subject. And I will also tell you how to contact individuals and organizations that can expand your knowledge and help you develop the confidence you will need to build the financial fortress that can give you and your family lifelong financial security.

April 1996

Arnold S. Goldstein, J.D., LL.M., Ph.D.
Arnold S. Goldstein & Associates, PA
384 S. Military Trail
Deerfield Beach, Florida 33442
954-420-4990

1

THE ULTIMATE FINANCIAL PROTECTION SYSTEM

More lawsuits. More government seizures. More lost privacy. More confiscatory taxes. More news of a faltering U.S. economy. Your wealth is in danger. Serious danger. That's why the world's finest legal and financial minds created the WealthSaver Trust that is revolutionizing financial planning for every concerned American.

The WealthSaver Trust has become the financial foundation for Americans with wealth to protect, the intelligence and foresight to know it must be protected, and the knowledge that the WealthSaver Trust is the one best way to protect it! Those with a WealthSaver Trust are the liberated, "financially free" citizens. These are the people who are best equipped to survive financially.

Dr. Goldstein, what is a WealthSaver Trust?

A WealthSaver Trust is a special trust established in a foreign country with strict laws that protect the trust assets from lawsuits and creditors. It also enforces secrecy concerning the trust and provides a platform for international investing.

You may know the WealthSaver Trust by several other names: the Offshore Asset Protection Trust (OAPT), Creditor Protection Trust, Offshore Trust, International Trust, Asset Conservation Trust or Foreign Trust.

The WealthSaver Trust® is my registered trademark for my own improved version of the standard offshore Asset Protection Trust. The WealthSaver Trust offers several features and improvements over the standard asset protection trust to produce an *even more powerful* wealth-conservation system. The name "WealthSaver®" is also more appropriate for this versatile financial weapon because the more common name "asset protection trust" overlooks the many other important benefits that one can obtain from this trust.

Why do you refer to the WealthSaver Trust as "the ultimate financial protection system?"

The WealthSaver Trust *is* the ultimate system to protect wealth because it does it *more* effectively than any other financial device available today. Some examples:

- *Asset protection?* The WealthSaver Trust can bullet-proof your assets from lawsuits and creditors and keep them safer than any other asset protector yet designed.

- *Confidentiality and secrecy?* This is always important to financial security, and the WealthSaver Trust superbly protects financial privacy in what is now a very public world.

- *More profitable investing and economic diversification?* To protect wealth you must avoid economic erosion to your wealth. The WealthSaver Trust excels here also.

While these benefits are common reasons for forming a WealthSaver Trust, there are many other benefits:

- forced heirship law avoidance

- premarital planning

- tax avoidance and deferral

- estate planning

- Medicaid planning and entitlement preservation

- avoidance of exchange controls

- international business planning

- regulatory avoidance

How new is the WealthSaver Trust?

The WealthSaver Trust is a relatively new twist to the trust's long heritage. Only within the past few years have certain foreign countries enacted special asset protection trust laws that allowed for the development of the WealthSaver Trust as the essential financial tool that it is today. Most WealthSaver Trusts have been established in this decade. However, it is fast becoming one of the most popular trusts. There are an increasing number of books, articles and seminars on this trust, and many more lawyers, accountants and financial planners are now familiar with it. More importantly, more recommend it to their clients.

Over $2.5 *trillion* is now protected in offshore WealthSaver Trusts. That's *trillions,* not *billions*! That vast sum represents about three times what we

Americans spend each year for health care and twice what the IRS collects annually in taxes! So you cannot question the WealthSaver Trust's validity when it protects $2.5 *trillion* on the advice of some of the world's leading lawyers and financial experts.

WealthSaver Trusts will explode in popularity. More middle-class Americans will insist upon such trusts and very few of the wealthy can afford to go without one. Only one thing can slow U.S. wealth flowing into offshore WealthSaver Trusts: our own government awakening to the harsh reality that so many Americans prefer to shelter their wealth *outside* the United States.

What are the differences between an offshore WealthSaver Trust and an irrevocable domestic trust?

The WealthSaver Trust is very similar to the domestic irrevocable trust, except that the WealthSaver Trust includes several features that greatly expand its protective powers.

Most importantly is the distinction that the WealthSaver Trust *is* foreign. That is, the trust is formed in a foreign haven that provides special asset protection to the wealth within the trust. That one difference is critical. Comparable U.S. trusts often remain vulnerable to creditors. The WealthSaver Trust is much less vulnerable and creditors can almost never reach its assets. This one advantage is the reason behind most WealthSaver Trusts. Other features also distinguish the WealthSaver Trust:

- *Foreign law governing.* The laws of the country where the trust is established govern the enforcement and interpretation of rights concerning the trust. These laws are *always* debtor-oriented.

- *Anti-duress provisions.* If a U.S. court compels the grantor to repatriate trust assets, the trustee must refuse this request.

- *Flight provisions.* These provisions compel or authorize the trustee to relocate the trust to another trust haven if the trust became endangered in its present location.

- *Discretionary powers.* These give the trustee full authority to decide a number of issues, including the payment of distributions to beneficiaries. This provision *may* be contained in a domestic trust.

- *Provisions to alter or terminate beneficial rights.* The trustee can alter the rights of any beneficiary under creditor attack to eliminate claims against the trust by that creditor.

- *Provisions for a protector.* These allow the appointment of individuals to oversee the trustee.

Many more subtle features characterize the WealthSaver Trust. These will be discussed later in greater detail. In sum, the WealthSaver Trust compares to domestic trusts the way a modern jet compares to a World War I biplane. They both fly but at considerably different speeds, altitudes and levels of performance.

Who are the people who are establishing WealthSaver Trusts?

Americans from every background are establishing WealthSaver Trusts. Most of my WealthSaver Trust clients are high-risk professionals and business people. As you would imagine, physicians lead the group, followed closely by lawyers, developers, real estate owners, corporate officers and directors, and, of course, the entrepreneurs. These people are chiefly looking for asset protection against lawsuits and creditor claims. Many have recently earned "windfalls" from their business and now want to protect their nest egg from claims. We are now frequently forming these trusts to protect business assets.

The second group seems more concerned with privacy. These are not people engaged in crimes or tax evasion, but only ordinary Americans who want more secrecy for their financial and personal affairs.

Lately, I see more clients using the WealthSaver Trust for estate and divorce planning purposes. Sometimes they only want secrecy from family members, but it often is to discourage litigation relating to inheritances or to protect assets in forthcoming marriages.

Still others want a platform for international investing. While these people could as well invest globally from less costly and less complicated offshore companies, they apparently want the protection for their investments which only the WealthSaver Trust can provide.

Most disturbing is the vast number of people who have no specific or immediate reason for establishing their trust. Their motives are more political or even ideological. Whether it is only their lost confidence in the American system, the WealthSaver Trust is often an expression of discontent at home. More than a few are planning to become exiles and are now expatriating their wealth as a prelude to renouncing their U.S. citizenship.

Is the WealthSaver Trust mostly for the wealthy?

Great wealth is not needed to benefit from your own WealthSaver Trust. A modest nest egg of $100,000 or less can well-justify the investment. The WealthSaver Trust becomes essential when you have considerably more assets at risk. Your "deep pockets" then make you a prime target for litigants and others who want your wealth. With significant wealth you need the most powerful protection possible. That, of course, is the WealthSaver Trust!

In a very real sense it is the mainline American — not the super rich — who most need the WealthSaver Trust. The super-rich may have greater ability to replenish their wealth while few middle-class Americans ever recoup from a financial catastrophe.

I have read many articles about offshore trusts that suggest a $500,000 or $1 million net worth makes such a trust worthwhile. But I disagree. It's smarter to establish your WealthSaver Trust *before* you accumulate considerable wealth because you want the trust to protect your wealth *as you accumulate it*. That's when the trust is most valuable. Moreover, you will not then establish the WealthSaver Trust as an afterthought when you are running from liabilities. You will instead have properly pre-planned your wealth protection.

Who are the parties to the WealthSaver Trust?

The WealthSaver Trust, as with any trust, must include

three essential parties:

- *The grantor* (or the settlor, donor or trustor) creates and funds the trust, appoints the initial trustees and names the beneficiaries.

- *The trustee* is appointed by the grantor and manages the trust for the benefit of the beneficiaries.

- *The beneficiaries* benefit from the trust and receive the trust's income and/or assets.

The WealthSaver Trust may also include:

- *An investment advisor* to recommend appropriate investments for the trust assets.

- *A custodian bank* to serve as the repository for the trust funds.

The WealthSaver Trust, unlike U.S. trusts, will also normally include:

- *A protector* to oversee the trustee.

I will later discuss their respective roles and how you can find, select and work effectively with each of these participants.

Who is usually the grantor?

The party who has the funds to invest is, of course, the grantor. It can be anyone. I have created WealthSaver

Trusts for grandparents seeking to protect their wealth for their grandchildren; husbands and wives who as co-grantors combined their wealth into one trust; and still other couples who established separate trusts with each spouse the grantor of his or her own trust. Which family member(s) becomes the grantor usually depends upon complex tax, asset protection, estate planning and even business considerations.

For confidentiality purposes you may prefer to have an offshore corporation or a foreign lawyer establish your trust and act as the nominee grantor. You can later fund the trust. To discourage fraudulent transfer claims, a debtor-husband may, for instance, transfer his funds to his wife who then becomes the sole grantor. Many WealthSaver Trusts do not name the grantor. Many jurisdictions do not require the recording of the trust document. The grantor's identity can in both instances remain undisclosed.

The grantor must own the property to be transferred to the trust and have full legal capacity and authority to transfer the assets. The grantor also must have the intent to form the trust.

Selecting the correct grantor is important because the trustee will be guided by the grantor who may influence the direction of the trust to the exclusion, for instance, of a spouse who would not share that control unless she was a co-grantor. The "proper" grantor is one of the first points you will discuss with your attorney.

Who Is appointed the trustee?

Selecting the right trustee(s) is particularly important because the trustee completely controls the trust.

As the grantor you should never be the sole trustee of your WealthSaver Trust. You must appoint at least one foreign trustee. A U.S. grantor, or any other American, can initially serve as a co-trustee, but should immediately resign his or her trusteeship once the trust comes under creditor attack. A common arrangement is to start with a committee of three trustees — an American husband and wife, for instance, and a foreign trustee. Pending creditor problems, the husband and wife would control the trusteeship, and they would resign only when a problem arises. The foreign trustee would then remain as the sole trustee.

WealthSaver Trusts always start with at least one foreign trustee. This is usually a resident from within the trust haven because that is commonly required. This also explains why you cannot substitute a foreign trustee only when under legal duress but must appoint one from the trust's inception.

Foreign trustees are plentiful and professionally qualified to administer WealthSaver Trusts as well as provide a variety of related offshore services. Most foreign trustees are chartered accountants or attorneys who passed a special examination. Some trustees work independently; however, you may prefer a larger trust company or be still more comfortable with a long-established bank as your institutional trustee. You can find a well-established trustee to serve you wherever you establish your trust. Later we will discuss how to find and choose *your* right trustee.

Your trustee *may* be selected from a country other than the trust haven. Several havens require local trustees; however, to satisfy their residency requirements, trustees elsewhere simply incorporate there.

How are the beneficiaries selected and designated?

Beneficiaries are those whom you want the trust to benefit during your lifetime or who will inherit the trust assets after your death. You select beneficiaries to a WealthSaver Trust in the same manner as under your will or living trust.

However, with a living trust, you would usually name yourself the sole lifetime beneficiary, but as grantor of a WealthSaver Trust you should not be the only beneficiary if you want creditor-protection.

The beneficiaries can be specifically named or

identified by category or class. For example, you may designate the beneficiaries as "all your surviving children in equal shares."

Frequently, the WealthSaver Trust names as the beneficiary a charity such as the International Red Cross or Salvation Army. This is immediately superseded by a "memorandum of wishes" from the grantor to the trustee requesting a substitution of beneficiaries. Within this memorandum you would designate your true beneficiaries. Since this is only a "request," the trustee can always decide *not* to honor the request concerning a particular beneficiary if that beneficiary has creditor problems.

The trust will specifically exclude certain parties from the status of beneficiaries. Creditors or other parties with an interest adverse to the grantor, or the trust generally, cannot be a beneficiary or occupy any other position in respect to the trust.

You can always request a change of beneficiaries; however, since the WealthSaver Trust is discretionary, whether to accept a change of beneficiaries is strictly within the trustee's discretion. Requests to change beneficiaries is, of course, normally honored by the trustee.

There are many creative ways to use the WealthSaver Trust for estate planning and to name beneficiaries to maximize the WealthSaver Trust's tax and legal advantages. Not only can you designate beneficiaries by name or by descriptive class but the beneficiaries also can be natural persons, profit or non-profit corporations, associations, partnerships, other trusts or any other legal entity, whether American or foreign. As the grantor you may designate beneficiaries and expand, contract, terminate or shift beneficial interests — subject only to trustee agreement.

What is the role of the trust protector?

The protector, like the trustee, protects the interests of the beneficiaries. The protector more specifically prevents misdeeds by the trustee.

The protector can only veto trustee decisions or those actions that appear inappropriate to the protector. The protector cannot force the trustee to undertake an act but can *prevent* trustee actions. For example, a trustee requires protector approval to sell trust investments or withdraw funds from the trust accounts, with or without grantor approval. The protector usually verifies grantor approval. The protector thus ensures that the trustee acts in the best interests of the grantor and the beneficiaries.

The protector's one most important power is his authority to replace the trustees. It is through the grantor's authority to change protectors, and the protector's authority to change trustees, that the grantor indirectly controls the trustee *and* the trust. The WealthSaver Trust will, however, require that the replacement trustee be independent of any grantor or beneficiary and someone not appointed by any court or creditor.

You can be the protector of your own trust. And most havens do not require a WealthSaver Trust to have a protector. However, serving as protector of your trust may encourage a U.S. court to decide that you control the trust and thus force you to repatriate trust assets to satisfy creditors. You can resign as protector when problems arise and then leave the trust without a protector, or you can appoint a successor protector. In my view, a grantor should *not* be his own trust protector. Spouses, other relatives, business associates or professional advisors are suitable. I prefer foreign protectors for the same reason I insist upon foreign trustees: to place the protector beyond the reach of an American creditor's subpoena and his power to examine under oath.

Larger trusts sometimes utilize protector committees consisting of three protectors and allowing any two to act. The committee may include a foreign trust company, a foreign bank and a domestic protector (usually the grantor's relative, associate or friend). Most WealthSaver Trusts cannot cost-justify a protector committee, which adds considerable expense and makes trust administration quite clumsy. You should, however, name successor protectors if the initial protector is unable or unwilling to serve.

The protector asserts considerable control over the trustee, and therefore greatly influences trust matters. Therefore, appointing the protector requires no less thought than naming the trustee.

The grantor, or one holding a power of appointment, initially appoints the protector and can change protectors with or without cause.

In what countries can you establish a WealthSaver Trust?

While there are numerous offshore havens, tax havens or financial centers, only a few have enacted trust legislation. Other jurisdictions have so-called common-law trusts, and therefore recognize trusts only through case law. Other countries have civil law trusts. These jurisdictions do not directly recognize the concept of a trust; however, an enforceable trust can result through the application of other laws. For Americans, the most popular WealthSaver Trust havens include the Cayman Islands, Bahamas, Belize, Cook Islands, Turks and Caicos and Nevis. There are, however, a number of other havens where WealthSaver Trusts are formed.

Cyprus, Malta, Gibraltar, Barbados, Isle of Man, Guernsey, Jersey and Seychelles are examples. We will later discuss each haven and explain the numerous factors you should consider when selecting the haven that would be best for your WealthSaver Trust.

How do you structure and organize the trust?

The trust usually conducts its affairs through an International Business Corporation (IBC). The trust then only owns this one asset, the entire shares of the IBC.

The IBC serves four important purposes: First, the trust can more easily trade and do business through an operating company (IBC). Second, the IBC insulates the trust from potential liabilities. Third, the IBC creates another layer of privacy. Fourth, the IBC helps avoid U.S. income tax liability on most U.S. source investment income.

The IBC is usually set up in a different haven than the trust haven, a country with favorable company laws. The Bahamas, British Virgin Islands or Seychelles are common choices. The trustee usually serves as the nominee-director of the IBC and manages the entire offshore system — the trust and IBC — as one entity. I often speak of the trust when in actuality it is the corporation owned by the trust that conducts the activities I refer to. This distinction is unimportant in our discussion.

Limited liability companies (LLCs) are now increasingly becoming substituted for the IBC for tax reasons. It is also common to have the WealthSaver Trust structured with a domestic family limited partnership or even domestic corporations and other trusts. The structural possibilities are endless and involve many tax, asset protection and other legal and financial considerations that are best left to your offshore professionals.

What assets are ordinarily transferred to the WealthSaver Trust?

To answer that you must first answer three questions: 1) What assets do you own? 2) What are your objectives with the WealthSaver Trust? 3) What are the legal threats, restrictions or contingencies?

For maximum asset protection, you would title whatever is possible in the WealthSaver Trust. This is the *in toto* approach. More often, only "nest egg" assets — cash, CDs, stocks and bonds — are held in trust. Cars, boats and personal homes are usually not held in trust because of fiduciary or tax considerations. But I have successfully sheltered *every* personal and family asset in a WealthSaver Trust with the objective that absolutely *nothing* remains exposed to creditors. Quite frequently, people invest only a small portion of their "nest egg" until they become more comfortable with the trust. They add assets as they develop confidence that the trust will perform to their satisfaction.

Some assets, for legal reasons, cannot be transferred to the trust. Retirement accounts (401K plans, IRAs and Keoughs) are examples. However, even these may possibly be transferred if you have a carefully designed special purpose trust. The trust also cannot own restricted stock or shares in an S corporation. The trustee also may refuse certain assets — particularly those that are burdensome to manage or likely to create liability.

You will also prefer to maintain control over certain assets — such as your home — and therefore will want to keep this in your name. Even then you may refinance your home and other U.S. assets and transfer the loan proceeds to the trust. Through this procedure, you can strip the equity in your U.S. assets and thus protect the asset without creating complications for the trustee, forfeiting control or losing tax benefits. Whether through direct transfer or equity stripping, you can effectively relocate and protect your *entire* wealth offshore.

How do you transfer assets to the trust?

This process is simple and involves the same procedures you use to transfer assets to any other entity. To transfer funds, you can, for instance, wire transfer or mail a check to your trustee. Your stockbroker can directly transfer your securities. You can transfer your personal property through a bill of sale or an assignment of rights. Real estate is conveyed by deed. We can transfer even a sizeable estate in a few hours of professional time.

What provisions are common in the standard WealthSaver Trust?

The WealthSaver Trust is a formidable document. As with all trusts, it will delineate the rights and responsibilities of the usual parties to the trust: the grantor, trustee, protector and beneficiaries. A well-constructed trust document can easily consist of 50 to 75 detailed pages and it will attempt to cover every contingency, particularly those intended to protect the trust assets from adversaries. My usual trust contains upwards of 80 separate provisions, and certainly a:

- *Settlement clause* where the grantor states his wishes for the life tenants and trust remaindermen.

- *Interpretation clause* for all trust terms.

- *Abeyance period clause* where during times of duress the grantor may divest himself of any interest in the trust.

- *Declaration of trust* whereby the grantor details and limits the power of the trustee.

- *Power to change beneficiaries clause* where the grantor (by prior written consent to the trustees) may add certain classes of beneficiaries.

- *Trustees compensation clause.*

- *Change of trustees clause,* which provides for the resignation and change of trustees.

- *Emergency provisions clause* which provides for new trustees in a fleeing jurisdiction to begin upon the occurrence of certain circumstances.

- *Trustees' indemnity clause* which limits trustees liability.

- *Investment management clause* which details how the trustees shall distribute and invest income and principal.

- *Irrevocability of trust clause.*

- *Additional powers and provisions clause.*

- *Power to appropriate clause,* which gives the trustees the power to appropriate principal to satisfy the terms of the settlement deed.

- *Spendthrift clause* which protects beneficial interests from creditors.

- *Discretionary clause* which provides the trustee the authority to act or not act.

- *Exercise of trustee powers* whereby trustees are authorized to exercise voting power (if multiple trustees), and corporate trustees are conferred discretionary powers.

- *Payments to beneficiaries clause,* authorizing payments to beneficiaries.

The overriding purpose of any WealthSaver Trust is to give the trustee, subject to protector approval, sweeping authority to deal with the assets to the complete exclusion of the grantor.

What control does the trustee have over the trust assets?

The trustee, subject to protector approval, has unlimited control and the full discretion to manage all trust assets. The trust thus allows the trustee to do whatever the trustee may foreseeably need to do to protect or enhance the trust assets. This includes all the common powers found in an irrevocable domestic trust — the right to sell, buy, lease, encumber or invest the assets; the right to defend or prosecute claims; the right to pay debts and taxes; the right to hire other professionals; and the right to make loans and/or distribute income or principal to beneficiaries.

As stated earlier, a unique protective feature of the WealthSaver Trust is the trustee's power to establish a successor trust with an emergency trustee in another haven if the trust becomes threatened.

The WealthSaver Trust purposely grants the trustee broad powers, and the grantor negligible authority. If the grantor has more control, the trust will lose its effectiveness as an asset protector. Admittedly, delegating complete control over your wealth to a foreign trustee can be frightening if you are a grantor, but it will be much less so once you realize how readily the trustee will comply with your wishes concerning trust matters.

The grantor concerned about control can take a number of intermediate measures to balance asset protection against the desire to retain control. Of course, your attorney must ultimately decide the control that you can safely retain without jeopardizing asset protection, but only after thoroughly investigating the actual or potential claims against you.

If delegating complete control to the trustee greatly concerns you, consider several options: You can appoint a protector you know will follow your directions. Since the protector can replace the trustee, you gain *alter ego* control. You also can make the trust *revocable* until a specified event occurs — such as a creditor lawsuit. The trust would then automatically become irrevocable. Or you may form a limited partnership that would primarily be owned by the WealthSaver Trust. As the general partner, you would control the limited partnership assets here in the U.S. until under legal duress when the partnership assets would be transferred to the offshore trust. You may also be the managing director of the IBC that is owned by the trust. You can also control the trusteeship until it is threatened by creditors, by having your spouse, or another U.S. designee, serve with you as co-trustees. Another option is to have your protector be a co-signor with the trustee on all trust accounts. Finally, you can leave your trust lightly funded until full expatriation of your wealth is necessary for asset protection. There are other control-retention techniques.

There are many safeguards to insure that your assets will always be handled as you wish. Real comfort will come from the fact that the foreign trustees will routinely exercise their discretionary powers to fulfill your every legal and reasonable request or wish as the grantor.

How does the grantor communicate his requests or "wishes" to the trustee?

The grantor may send to the trustee a letter, statement or memorandum of wishes, or a "side letter," that will contain the grantor's requests concerning matters of trust structure or administration. The grantor can, for instance, request a change of beneficiaries, new investments, a loan to himself or another beneficiary, or even the appointment of a new trustee and/or protector. So while the trustee appears to have full *legal* control and the grantor *no* apparent authority, the grantor, in fact, retains considerable *de facto* control over the trust as foreign trustees will acquiesce to a grantor's reasonable requests or find that they have no future as a trustee. It is even understood that a trustee will step aside in favor of a new trustee at the request of a grantor.

How safe are assets entrusted to a foreign trustee?

This is the most common question I am asked and certainly it is a big concern for my clients. When someone, particularly a stranger on another continent, fully controls *your* money, you become rightfully concerned that the trustee may embezzle, squander or lose your money on bad investments.

Fortunately, there is very little basis for this concern. Foreign trustees have an impeccable track record for honesty and prudence. In fact, I have not heard of *one* instance where *any* American has *ever* lost money due to theft by a foreign trustee. Foreign trustees are professionals. More importantly, they are, or should be, fully bonded. Moreover, they are inevitably backed by the reputation of their own countries. An offshore haven cannot afford an embezzlement scandal. Their haven would necessarily make restitution if one of their trustees proved dishonest. Your protector can also safeguard your money by becoming a co-signer on your trust accounts. Finally, selecting a bank with an 800-year reputation for honesty in the handling of other people's money should, in the final analysis, dispel all concerns.

It is nevertheless necessary to choose a foreign trustee with diligence. However, as a general proposition, you have considerably more safeguards with a foreign trustee than you do with a U.S. trustee.

How are the trust funds invested?

While the trust will provide that the trustee selects the investments, the trustee will normally invest as you wish — if your investments are acceptable for trusts. Whether you are an active or passive investor, your trustee will follow your investment recommendations. And you can invest anywhere in the world where your money will be safe from creditors.

You probably will not invest in the country where the trust is located because you want the very best global investments, and these usually do not originate in these small havens. Whether it is Swiss annuities, a Liechtenstein bank account, gold bullion stored in Austria, a blue-chip German mutual fund or an array of other international investments — you shape your portfolio. Your WealthSaver Trust will give you the opportunity to invest anywhere and in any type of investment. You will soon discover how profitable and exciting the international investment market can be.

If the WealthSaver Trust is irrevocable, how are its assets eventually repatriated to the United States?

As the grantor you cannot repatriate your funds by revoking or dissolving the trust, but there are alternate ways to access the trust funds. One way is to borrow from the trust, which is permitted if you are a beneficiary. You can do this either directly or by having the trust collateralize a loan for you from a local bank through a "back-to-back" loan. Your trust also can transact business with you, or your company. This indirectly diverts funds back to you. The trustee can also make distributions to any beneficiary, including yourself if you are a beneficiary. If you are not a beneficiary, your spouse and children probably will be. Trust distributions to them can in turn be gifted or loaned to you. As you can see, there are many ways to access whatever funds you need and whenever they are needed. You can, usually within 48 hours, have whatever funds you need back in your own pocket.

You also *can* provide that your trust is revocable with the assent of both the trustee and the protector. The grantor cannot directly exercise a right or revocation or the trust will then lose its asset protection benefits. However, if the trustee and protector revoke the trust, the assets will revert to the grantor.

What happens to the trust and the trust assets when the grantor dies?

The trust assets will then normally be distributed according to the trust provisions. The final beneficiaries and provisions for distribution are normally through a letter of wishes or a series of side letters that reflect changes the grantor periodically desires.

The WealthSaver Trust is usually an *inter vivos* trust, that is it operates during the grantor's lifetime. But it can also become a *testamentary* trust and continue beyond your lifetime for the benefit of remaining beneficiaries on terms the grantor specifies. The WealthSaver Trust can, and often is, drafted to smoothly and efficiently transfer the grantor's wealth to his designated heirs. The WealthSaver Trust, as you will see, is a remarkably versatile estate planning tool.

The trust ordinarily provides that it will dissolve upon the grantor's death or after a set number of years. The term can be extended at the grantor's election or extended automatically if the grantor should have problems and wants continued protection from the trust. If the grantor were alive upon the termination of the trust, the assets would revert to him. If termination occurs upon or after his death, the assets would go to the remainder beneficiaries that he previously named.

Considering the WealthSaver Trust's many benefits, why do so few Americans know about it?

One reason is that we Americans remain hoodwinked by the IRS, American bankers and other pro-establishment groups with their own self-serving reasons for perpetuating the myths about offshore finance. The gullible still believe offshore havens are evil, dangerous and illegal — despite the fact that nearly *every* Fortune-500 company has offshore business or financial interests, as do eight of the top ten U.S. banks. Even our own U.S. government is heavily invested offshore. Offshore finance is not only legal and ethical but it's also absolutely smart. Still, most Americans *don't* understand the world of offshore finance. They instead believe only what they read or hear from a controlled media too ready to paint offshore havens as a hangout for tax evaders, money launderers, crooks and other scofflaws. Nor does it stop there. Parochial-thinking lawyers, accountants and financial planners do little to give their clients the correct facts — if *they* should know them. Americans are insular. We are far less sophisticated about international finance than are, for instance, Londoners or others who live at the crossroads of international finance.

The fear, negativity and plain ignorance that surrounds offshore finance results largely from misinformation. But I say, Americans are slowly awakening. We are learning. More and more see how their friends, relatives and associates have found *their* financial freedom with the WealthSaver Trust. You cannot stop a good idea whose time has come. And it *is* the time for the WealthSaver Trust. In the following pages, you will see the many reasons why!

WEALTHSAVER HIGHLIGHTS

• The WealthSaver Trust is *revolutionizing* financial planning. Over $2.5 *trillion* is now invested in these trusts, and it is escalating rapidly.

• The WealthSaver Trust offers numerous benefits: asset protection, privacy, possible tax advantages, probate avoidance, sound estate planning, plus the opportunity to *build* wealth with superior international investments.

• The WealthSaver Trust is not only for the rich. It is for *anyone* with *any* wealth to conserve!

• Your funds are safe and well-protected if you correctly choose a foreign trustee. And there are many ways to build even *more* protection.

- Your trustee *must* control the trust; however, your trustee will normally acquiesce to your wishes.

- As the grantor, you can recommend how the trust assets are to be invested, and through your requests even change the trustee or beneficiaries.

- While the WealthSaver Trust is irrevocable, you *can* reclaim your funds in several ways.

2

BUILDING YOUR OFFSHORE FINANCIAL FORTRESS

*W*ho *can feel financially secure in our lawsuit-crazy, seizure-mad, tax-happy, own-it-today, lose-it-tomorrow world? Consider these sad facts:*

Nearly 60 million lawsuits are filed annually in the United States. Twenty million Americans now owe the IRS hefty back taxes. One in two couples get divorced. Arbitrary, capricious governmental seizures are the new-wave threat. RICO and other draconian laws empower federal and state governments to freely grab your assets.

The ways you can lose your assets are indeed endless. In our high-risk society, the challenge is not making money, but keeping it! Those who survive this financial maelstrom will need a lawsuit-proof, creditor-proof financial fortress. That will be the WealthSaver Trust.

Dr. Goldstein, are most WealthSaver Trusts primarily established for asset protection?

Unquestionably. Asset protection is my professional specialty, and I am absolutely swamped by clients frightened they will lose their wealth. Whether their concern is lawsuits, the IRS, creditors, ex-spouses or any of the 1,001 other potential threats to their pocketbooks, they have good reason to worry. Only people with absolutely no assets can ignore asset protection. Four out of five clients who come to me for WealthSaver Trusts primarily want asset protection, so that's certainly its most powerful benefit and biggest selling point.

I also notice that people are establishing their WealthSaver Trusts earlier in the game. They no longer wait until they are in deep financial trouble before they protect themselves. They want WealthSaver Trust protection today because they rightfully fear what may happen to them *tomorrow*. This defensive financial planning is essential *now*. It will be more essential in the years ahead. The fear of losing your wealth to forces beyond your control is what drives the WealthSaver Trust boom and that fear will continue to drive it.

Before we discuss the WealthSaver Trust's asset protection powers, what do you mean by asset protection?

Asset protection is the process of shielding your wealth against future danger. Mostly we mean against lawsuits and creditors. The broader definition includes wealth erosion through such economic hazards as inflation, deflation or taxes. That's not what I'm talking about here, although the WealthSaver Trust can help in tax-planning and insure greater economic stability through global investing. But for now I am talking about protection against more deliberate predators — litigants, the tax collector, creditors, ex-spouses. These predatory dangers now greatly eclipse the economic hazards to your wealth.

Are lawsuits the chief concern and reason to protect assets? And why do we have so much litigation in America?

The litigation explosion is partly because we are now swamped with lawyers who must manufacture lawsuits to keep busy. Too many lawsuits are frivolous or apparent extortions. We also have many expanded theories of liability. For example, consider how many more lawsuits Congress created with the Civil Rights Act. Judges and juries forget their rightful role and become modern-day Robin Hoods, robbing the rich to give to the poor — even without establishing liability. And traditional forms of protection no longer work well. Corporations, for example, are too easily pierced. Bankruptcy extinguishes fewer debts. Insurance covers fewer claims. All this increased exposure compels greater asset protection.

The litigation explosion, of course, results from numerous legal, economic, political and social trends. Whatever the cause, we are no longer the simple, trusting and friendly people we once were. In our complex, hostile, predatory world, you are forced to litigate to only stay even — if not get ahead.

So lawsuits are the chief concern for most individuals and businesses, and it is what spurs asset protection as a mushrooming legal specialty. The WealthSaver Trust was created *only* because we have so many lawsuits. It is the asset protection lawyer's big weapon to duel plaintiffs armed with runaway laws, sympathetic juries and greedy lawyers.

In what ways does the WealthSaver Trust discourage litigation?

The WealthSaver Trust discourages litigation in three ways. First, the WealthSaver Trust provides secrecy for your wealth. You no longer advertise your "deep pockets." This will stop many potential lawsuits before they even start.

Second, the WealthSaver Trust should convince even the most determined plaintiff that he would find it difficult if not impossible to collect, whether or not a lawsuit is under way. This provides the leverage you need to settle cheaply.

Third, the judgment creditor could not in the final analysis seize your assets. You thus have the protection you want even if a creditor does successfully press his claim.

How effectively does the WealthSaver Trust discourage litigation?

The fastest, surest way to stop our litigation explosion is for more Americans to protect their assets. When you can't get your neighbor's money, you don't try.

The wealthy — those with the deepest pockets — are prime lawsuit targets. Prospective litigants know that they will rather pay than fight because it's cheaper. Who can afford today's exorbitant lawyer's fees? Who can risk a devastating outcome in a "crapshoot" court?

Asset protection levels the playing field. The defendant gains bargaining leverage because the plaintiff cannot collect from him even if he sues and wins. That's incentive enough for any sensible plaintiff to settle early and inexpensively.

Isn't it smarter to conceal the WealthSaver Trust from creditors?

The WealthSaver Trust does not protect assets through secrecy. Nor will disclosing offshore wealth invested in one of these trusts detract from the trust's protection. That's why the WealthSaver Trust is your best *legal* alternative if you want solid protection without *illegally* concealing your endangered assets. The fact that the creditor knows about your trust will give him no better claim to its assets. With the trust, you can be both *truthful* and *safe*. If you only bury your money in a coffee can in your backyard or squirrel your money in an offshore bank account, you can stay safe only if you are *dishonest*.

How does the WealthSaver Trust protect assets from lawsuits and creditors? What makes it so powerful a wealth protector?

The WealthSaver Trust protects assets three ways: First, the WealthSaver Trust is set up in a country that neither recognizes nor enforces U.S. judgments or judicial or administrative orders — such as from the IRS. You thus enjoy complete jurisdictional immunity.

Second, the WealthSaver Trust is an irrevocable, discretionary trust. When someone other than the grantor is the trustee, the grantor no longer controls the trust assets. Therefore, the grantor's future creditors have no legal right or access to the trust assets.

Third, the WealthSaver Trust has several unique anti-duress, anti-creditor provisions that add considerable protection. Generally, they allow the trust assets to be maneuvered so that a creditor has no practical way to reach them.

Let's start with the first point — selecting a country for the WealthSaver Trust that will not enforce U.S. judgments or decrees. Which havens do enforce American judgments?

Many countries enforce American judgments or court orders. They are all worthless for asset protection. Others partly cooperate with American law enforcement, whether through treaty, such as Mutual Legal Assistance Treaties (MLAT), or through "comity," a reciprocal recognition of the judicial decrees of another country. In fact, very few countries completely ignore the legal orders of another country. With a WealthSaver Trust you only want a country that will not enforce U.S. *civil* decrees.

A WealthSaver Trust haven that won't recognize an American civil decree forces the creditor to re-litigate its case within the haven. However, this may be impossible or impractical because the statute of limitations for commencing suit has expired, the haven will not recognize the legal claim, or other procedural obstacles block litigation. Trust havens are extremely debtor-oriented. They must strive hard to protect because protection is what they sell.

Can a WealthSaver Trust protect your assets once you have a claim against you?

The WealthSaver Trust is your *safest* alternative once somebody is already after you. Domestic trusts or other U.S. based asset protection structures or strategies are then too vulnerable. Transfers to domestic entities to hinder or delay existing creditors are recoverable. While it is as much a fraudulent transfer to shelter your money offshore under these same circumstances, nevertheless, it is the one transfer that your creditors cannot readily recover. The creditor's rights have not changed, only his power to enforce those rights has greatly diminished.

Never transfer assets offshore to avoid existing claims *without* first consulting an attorney experienced in asset protection. Lawyers, for legal or ethical reasons, may then refuse to protect you. While no lawyer can commit fraud, I believe too many lawyers confuse fraudulent conveyance with fraud. A fraudulent conveyance is neither a crime nor a tort (civil wrong). A fraudulent conveyance only gives the creditor the right to recover the transferred asset. Your lawyer, on one hand, must aggressively protect your assets without, on the other, crossing the line of illegality. A lawyer who does otherwise may be liable for malpractice. But when do you cross that line from aggressive representation to unethical or illegal practice? There is considerable debate in the legal profession concerning that line.

Your lawyer may ask you to sign an Affidavit of Solvency. This affirms that you do not have claims against you or that you will otherwise have sufficient assets to pay said claims. Its purpose is to protect the attorney, as well as the trustee and protector, from any claim that they knowingly participated in a fraudulent asset transfer. I continuously emphasize one point you constantly hear from all good lawyers: Protect your assets *before* you have problems.

If assets were fraudulently transferred to a WealthSaver Trust, couldn't the court then retransfer these trust assets to the creditor?

That's the one big advantage of an offshore WealthSaver Trust over domestic asset protection strategies. Assets fraudulently transferred to a domestic trust, or to some other entity within the U.S., *could* be recovered because a U.S. court still has jurisdiction over these assets. However, American courts have no jurisdiction over assets that are offshore. So, the WealthSaver Trust offers considerably more protection than will a U.S.-based arrangement which always remains susceptible to fraudulent transfer claims.

This is a very important point. You can never know when someone will raise a claim from the past, or when you will need the jurisdictional immunity only a foreign WealthSaver Trust can give you. Your domestic asset protection program is weak if you question whether it can withstand a fraudulent transfer claim. And there are very few instances where a creditor cannot at least argue that the liability predated the conveyance — and thus press the fraudulent conveyance issue. I don't want these arguments when I protect my clients' wealth. That inevitably leads me to a WealthSaver Trust that renders such arguments largely academic.

If an American court cannot recover fraudulently transferred offshore assets, can't it then compel the American judgment debtor to repatriate the WealthSaver Trust funds or face contempt?

While a U.S. judge cannot redirect the ownership of WealthSaver Trust assets that are beyond U.S. court jurisdiction, an American grantor-debtor *is* under the court's powers. However, a court *cannot* compel a debtor to do what the debtor has no legal power to do. Only the trustee has the power to return assets titled to the trust. By the trust terms, the grantor, as judgment-debtor, cannot compel his foreign trustee to return assets and therefore cannot be held in contempt for any failure to repatriate.

The WealthSaver Trust legally breaks the chain of legal ownership between the grantor and his assets. The "anti-duress" clause in the WealthSaver Trust further provides that the trustee *must* ignore any request from any grantor or beneficiary that is made under court order.

This is why only a WealthSaver Trust rather than an offshore account or offshore company can protect your assets in this situation. Because you directly control your offshore company and personal accounts, a U.S. court *can* then order you to repatriate funds in these self-controlled accounts under threat of contempt. The WealthSaver Trust chiefly protects the trust assets by insuring that no American court has power over either the trust assets or those who control the trust.

Does it help to defend against fraudulent transfer claims by demonstrating that you set up the trust for purposes other than asset protection?

This can be an important strategy if your trust is in one of the many havens where the creditor must actually prove fraudulent intent. The debtor may then want to position matters so that he can more successfully argue a purpose for the trust other than asset protection.

The debtor's attorney should at the least utilize the trust for estate planning purposes, and this should be well-documented. However, there can be other documented reasons for establishing the trust. Business reasons, avoidance of the forced heirship laws and confidentiality are the three most common.

If an American creditor cannot obtain recovery of the assets from a U.S. court, can't the creditor file a fraudulent transfer claim where the trust is established?

Possibly. However, the haven's trust laws will offer enormous debtor protection and feature several obstacles few creditors will even try to overcome. One example is a short statute of limitations. Claims, for instance, must usually be filed within one or two years from the trust's formation. Few creditors will be in a position to challenge the trust that quickly. The creditor also must *prove beyond a reasonable doubt* that it was a fraudulent conveyance. This is quite difficult. Several havens, such as Nevis, also require that the creditor post a sizeable cash bond before commencing litigation. The creditor also must hire local counsel who can be expensive and work on a fee-only basis. Only a most determined, well-heeled creditor who is chasing considerable assets would attempt to overcome these and so many other formidable hurdles. The specific hurdles, of course, vary among jurisdictions. Finally, an American creditor holding a U.S. judgment will most often have to re-litigate the case again within the haven and obtain a judgment from the haven before it can bring a second suit to set aside the trust as fraudulent.

Of course, no asset protection haven can completely disregard a creditors' rights to recover a fraudulent transfer. Its policy is only to make it difficult. *Exceptionally* difficult.

What would happen in a worst case scenario where some very determined creditor does pursue a fraudulent transfer to a WealthSaver Trust to the point where the haven may set aside the trust?

The WealthSaver Trust will then flex its mightiest muscle and relocate your trust assets to a new trust haven. This will force the creditor to begin a new legal proceeding in that second haven. Of course, the creditor will soon tire from the chase because the debtor can continuously move the trust assets to still other trust havens.

The flight provision is the WealthSaver Trust's most powerful asset protection feature because it essentially deprives the creditor of all practical possibilities of reaching the trust assets regardless of the legal proceedings he may initiate or their outcome. Whether a haven *would* give a creditor relief is of *no* consequence when no haven is ever given the opportunity!

Considering the many formidable obstacles a creditor faces, how many creditors actually attack a WealthSaver Trust?

The WealthSaver Trust's protection is most appreciated when you consider that fewer than three out of a hundred offshore trusts have been challenged. And these rare cases are typically settled as nuisance claims for pennies on the dollar. Without the WealthSaver Trust protection, these creditors would have undoubtedly recovered significantly more. The fact that 97 out of 100 creditors *won't* challenge a WealthSaver Trust strongly endorses its asset protection powers.

Of course, in a great number of cases the creditor had the *legal* right to recover assets. Any unwillingness to attempt a recovery is then founded on its *impracticality*. A creditor can spend enormous legal fees and never recover trust assets, even when it is within the creditor's legal right. As with many asset protection strategies, the goal is often to make it *impractical* for a creditor to pursue a claim, which in the case of the WealthSaver Trust is almost the same as *impossible*.

If the grantor's creditors cannot reach the trust's assets, can the beneficiaries' creditors?

The beneficiary's creditors have probably *less* power to reach trust assets. WealthSaver Trusts are discretionary trusts. This gives the beneficiaries no vested interests while the trustee enjoys wide discretion whether to distribute assets or income to the beneficiaries and, of course, the beneficiary's creditors.

For added protection the trust also contains a spendthrift provision that prevents a beneficiary's creditors from seizing the beneficiary's undistributed interest. Moreover, the trustee can refuse to recognize the individual as a beneficiary as this also would come within the discretionary powers. Obviously, the safest course is for an individual with creditors not to become a beneficiary until the creditor problems are resolved. Certain trusts automatically terminate a beneficial interest that is subject to creditor claim.

Can the WealthSaver Trust protect inheritances?

The WealthSaver Trust is a superb way to shield antic-ipated inheritances from the creditors of a beneficiary. First, the WealthSaver Trust can be a testamentary trust. Here, the inheritance would directly pass to the WealthSaver Trust upon the grantor's death. Or it can be an *inter vivos* trust and funded during the testator's lifetime. The WealthSaver Trust beneficiaries, in either case, would be protected against creditors through the trust's spendthrift provisions as well as the trustee's discretionary powers not to distribute princi-pal or interest to the beneficiaries — or specific beneficiaries — as I previously mentioned.

Can a bankruptcy trustee reach assets in the WealthSaver Trust?

A bankruptcy trustee has the same recovery powers as an individual creditor and, absent treaties to the con-trary, is equally powerless to reach the bankrupt's interest in a WealthSaver Trust.

If the bankrupt is one of multiple beneficiaries, the trustee of the trust is under no obligation to distrib-ute to the bankrupt beneficiary. If he decides to exclude a particular beneficiary from a distribution, or accumu-late income without a distribution, the bankruptcy trustee (or creditor) could not compel otherwise. This is why your WealthSaver Trust must be a true discretionary trust with at least two discretionary beneficiaries. The beneficiaries then have no vested interest in the trust property, but only an expectancy or possibility of an interest, which would not be vulnerable to a bankruptcy trustee or judgment creditor.

Therefore, a bankruptcy trustee has no unique ability to reach WealthSaver Trust assets. However, if the bankruptcy court determines that transfers to the trust were fraudulent, it may deny a bankruptcy discharge, either completely or to the value of the assets transferred. It is also essential to truthfully report to the bankruptcy court all recent transfers to the trust and any interest you may have in the trust. Dishonesty is bankruptcy fraud.

Of course, a bankruptcy trustee can pursue fraudulent transfers to the trust, subject to the same obstacles that other creditors face. This usually results in no recovery attempt or an advantageous settlement with the trustee.

When bankruptcy may be in your future, it becomes particularly important to pick the right trust haven. British Commonwealth havens, for example, are compelled under Section 426 of the United Kingdom Insolvency Act of 1986 to grant reciprocal enforcement of U.K. and Commonwealth bankruptcy decrees. A United States bankruptcy decree thus entered in the United Kingdom may be enforceable in a Commonwealth haven such as the Bahamas, Belize, Bermuda, British Virgin Islands, Cayman Islands, Gibraltar and Turks and Caicos. A trust haven also may not protect against foreign bankruptcies. This again will depend upon treaty arrangements. Of course, it is always possible to relocate the trust to a haven without reciprocal bankruptcy treaties in the eventuality of bankruptcy; however, the choice of haven is best decided before establishing the trust.

Can the WealthSaver Trust effectively protect assets against the IRS?

While more mortal creditors and litigants can usually be stonewalled by such domestic asset protectors as state homestead laws and exemption statutes, this is not so with the IRS. A taxpayer's assets are safest from IRS seizure *only when* they are sheltered offshore in a WealthSaver Trust. This is because most laws that safeguard assets against ordinary creditors will not protect against the IRS and probably other federal agencies.

WealthSaver Trust havens will not enforce an IRS levy or summons or cooperate with other IRS efforts to discover or seize trust assets. This is not necessarily true with other foreign havens that may have treaty arrangements with the U.S.

Taxpayers with serious IRS problems frequently sell or mortgage their assets and then transfer their liquidated wealth to their WealthSaver Trust, often steps ahead of a tax lien. As with bankruptcy, all asset transfers to the trust and legal or beneficial interests in the trust *must* be honestly disclosed to the IRS when it attempts enforced collection.

With so many marriages dissolving, is the WealthSaver Trust a popular way to protect assets in a divorce?

Unhappy spouses who contemplate divorce oftentimes shelter marital assets in WealthSaver Trusts. However, they must eventually and truthfully disclose these assets to the divorce court. While the divorce court cannot recover trust assets for division under the divorce, that hardly assures victory. The divorce court can award the victimized spouse a disproportionate share of the U.S. based assets to compensate for the trust-shielded assets. The court also can grant the injured spouse additional compensatory alimony or support. The WealthSaver Trust is best used to *protect* your share of the assets from a potentially dishonest spouse, not to cheat that spouse.

Dr. Goldstein, while the WealthSaver Trust apparently provides great protection, how much more protection than do other asset protection strategies?

If you have no present or anticipated claims against you, then several domestic asset protectors may work well for you:

- State homestead laws, to some degree, may protect your home.

- Unprotected investments can be converted to exempt or protected assets. Annuities and insurance, for instance, are sometimes protected from creditors by state law.

- Corporations and limited liability companies may hold assets safe from creditors, particularly Nevada and Wyoming corporations whose secrecy compares to the WealthSaver Trust.

- Domestic irrevocable trusts can safely hold assets. Caution: Revocable trusts provide *no* asset protection.

- Husbands and wives may own property as tenants-by-the-entirety or as community property. This often provides protection against one spouse's creditors.

- You may lever, mortgage or "equity-strip" your property to a more friendly creditor, leaving less-friendly creditors no equity to seize.

- Family limited partnerships are now enormously

popular for asset protection because they give you full control over the partnership assets while protecting against creditors. I prepare hundreds of FLPs each year because they are the foundation for *domestic* asset protection planning as the WealthSaver Trust is the foundation for *offshore* planning.

These possibilities only scratch the surface of what you can do to protect your wealth *within* the U.S. Unfortunately, these domestic asset protectors each have serious restrictions and limitations. Separately and collectively they offer you *less* protection than will the more formidable WealthSaver Trust, particularly when the creditor can claim a fraudulent transfer.

What assets can be protected through a WealthSaver Trust?

You can protect *any* asset; however, liquid, portable assets — cash, securities and even such collectibles as gold or jewelry — are most easily protected because you can physically relocate them outside the United States. Real estate or other onshore possessions, such as a car, boat or U.S. securities, will necessarily remain within U.S. jurisdiction and can then be recovered by U.S. courts if they are fraudulently conveyed to the trust. As your trustees and protectors should be foreign-based to remain beyond the reach of American courts, so should the trust assets.

Sheltering assets *outside* the U.S. becomes critical under a fraudulent transfer. The only way to protect tangible onshore assets against present creditors is to mortgage or sell the asset and expatriate the cash proceeds to the WealthSaver Trust. The American creditor's recourse is then only to an equity-stripped asset.

Can the WealthSaver Trust invest in U.S. securities, mutual funds or other American assets or will this reduce protection?

Some people hold their U.S. investments in their WealthSaver Trust until they are threatened by creditors and then exchange them for foreign investments. I recommend starting your WealthSaver Trust with foreign investments for three reasons. First, I consider offshore investments generally superior. Second, foreign trustees won't always invest in U.S. assets. Third, you never know when your assets are endangered. Avoid unpleasant surprises. You need not worry about surprise strikes when your assets are offshore.

It is important to locate such investments in jurisdictions where they will be protected. This excludes the U.S., Canada, England and many other countries with strong treaty arrangements with the United States.

WealthSaver Trust funds in American banks can easily be seized or frozen by U.S. creditors who can successfully claim a fraudulent transfer. Also avoid foreign banks with American branches because creditors can seize offshore WealthSaver Trust accounts through these branches. You must use *only* foreign banks and custodians with absolutely no presence in the United States.

Must the WealthSaver Trust be immediately funded or can it be delayed until there is a claim?

Many people delay the funding of their WealthSaver Trust until it is absolutely necessary. You also may want to continue with your current U.S. investments or simply may be more comfortable when your money is under *your* control.

The WealthSaver Trust accommodates this. One compromise strategy is to organize a U.S. limited partnership and have your WealthSaver Trust become a limited partner and own perhaps 99 percent of the partnership. As the 1-percent general partner you would manage the assets and decide if and when the partnership assets will be transferred to the trust. The partnership assets may never be distributed to the WealthSaver Trust nor leave the United States unless it is absolutely necessary. Until then, the partnership assets can remain with the partnership and under your full control.

A limited partnership combined with a WealthSaver Trust is formidable protection against a major lawsuit. Through these two entities you can straddle the fence. On one hand, you may not want your funds offshore *if* the lawsuit can be resolved. On the other hand, you cannot keep your assets exposed *if* you lose the case. Your assets would then remain in the partnership until there is a clear and present danger. The partnership assets then would be distributed to the partners. The WealthSaver Trust as the major partner would then transfer its partnership proceeds offshore beyond creditor reach.

Many more Americans now own offshore banks for asset protection. How do offshore banks compare to a WealthSaver Trust for asset protection purposes?

Owning your own offshore bank is an extremely effective way to add privacy to the WealthSaver Trust. Bank ownership makes it much more difficult for creditors to identify assets deposited to the bank's general fund because it becomes nearly impossible to link those funds to property or collateral obtained in exchange. Offshore banks are expected to widely invest their funds. Individuals are not.

How can funds be reclaimed from the WealthSaver Trust if there are still creditors?

Repatriated trust funds are, of course, always vulnerable to prowling creditors. Your objective with your WealthSaver Trust is to use it as your safe haven so you can negotiate a favorable settlement with your creditors, or go bankrupt on the claim — while preserving your wealth. This duress period usually lasts only a year or so, and you would not repatriate more funds than you would immediately need during this period.

During this period you have several options to safely access your trust funds: 1) Your WealthSaver trustee may directly pay your bills. 2) Funds may be repatriated to a domestic spendthrift trust which would disburse them for you. 3) You can transfer the repatriated funds to a third party account for temporary protection. 4) A spouse or other close relative can become a co-beneficiary and then receive and expend funds from the trust on your behalf.

These arrangements, while a temporary nuisance, generally do not present a major or long-term problem. Once your creditor problems vanish you can again repatriate your money without concern.

Dr. Goldstein, are there other tips on how to use the WealthSaver Trust to protect assets?

The asset protection possibilities with the WealthSaver Trust are endless. The versatile WealthSaver Trust can protect your assets in many, many additional ways. For instance, the WealthSaver Trust can loan you back your own money and encumber your U.S. assets to secure repayment. The mortgage can be so high and repayment terms so unattractive that creditors would not pursue the pledged asset. Since you indirectly control the trust you can always "adjust" the loan in ways to most effectively shield your U.S. assets.

An even smarter option is to borrow money from your trust through a shared appreciation mortgage. Here, you borrow money from the trust and agree to repay the loan at a lower interest rate in exchange for the trust receiving a share of the pledged property's future appreciation. This is a common WealthSaver Trust arrangement and one of my favorites. The profits eventually go to the trust, tax-deductible to you and tax-deferred until your death, while the shared appreciation mortgage shields future equity build-up from creditors.

We also have recently designed a formidable "friendly mortgage" arrangement whereby you can pledge your U.S. assets to the trust without *any* money changing hands. It is a solid plan that will withstand creditor challenge and involves guarantees from the trust annuity.

Does your business have accounts receivable? When trouble lurks you can sell the receivables to your trust for a big discount with several advantages: First, the difference between the discounted purchase price and the payments received by the trust can be tax-deferred until your death. Second, you can warrant the collectibility of the transferred receivables and encumber to the trust other unprotected U.S. assets to guarantee their collectibility. This combines long-term tax-deferral with excellent asset protection. Transferring receivables to the WealthSaver Trust at a huge discount quickly protects these vulnerable assets from creditors. U.S. courts routinely rule that about 50 cents on the dollar for the sale of receivables is fair consideration, and cash proceeds from the sale are far easier to protect from creditors than are slow-to-collect receivables.

Countless arrangements are possible between your offshore trust and your U.S.-based assets, and we are constantly devising newer and more creative asset protection arrangements.

Do you improve your protection by establishing more than one WealthSaver Trust?

If you have $5 million to put offshore you might set up five separate WealthSaver Trusts with five different trustees in five different havens. This certainly makes it more difficult for a creditor to reach the entire amount. It also is about five times more expensive to set up and maintain. There are tradeoffs. I seldom have clients invest more than $2 million in any one trust; however, this is my own arbitrary standard. You must decide for yourself how many of your eggs you want in any one basket.

Can an American be a trustee or protector of his own WealthSaver Trust or otherwise control the trust?

Once under creditor attack (duress), you should be neither a trustee nor protector of your own trust. You must then relinquish all control over the trust to a foreign-based trustee and protector who would both be beyond the jurisdiction of U.S. courts.

An important 1990 case, the Rahman decision, ruled that a WealthSaver Trust protects assets *only* if the grantor surrenders complete control and discretion to the trustee. The trustee cannot be a mere alter-ego or sham for the grantor. This is the trade-off.

Many of my clients read their trust completely astonished over their lack of control or decision-making authority. Their "knee-jerk" reaction is to bargain for more control while never realizing that the absence of control is what builds protection.

Creditors *will* scrutinize a trust arrangement to see if it is a sham that the courts can set aside. A sham transaction appears to create rights which are not intended to have legal effect.

You must remember that creditors have broad discovery powers and can oftentimes unravel a trust simply by showing that the grantor or beneficiaries made too many decisions concerning the trust. If the court concludes that the trustee is only the grantor's *alter ego*, the court is likely to declare the trust a legal fiction and dissolve it for the benefit of creditors. While you can make *requests* of your trustee, you cannot issue *commands* or otherwise do the trustee's job. Violate this sacred rule and you jeopardize the trust.

Here is the $64 million question about the WealthSaver Trust's asset-protection powers: Does it really succeed?

Prospective clients and other professionals ask me that some question almost daily. The answer depends on how you define "success."

We cannot guarantee that your WealthSaver Trust assets will never be pursued by a creditor. Nor can we guarantee that a creditor who does pursue your trust will not succeed — however rare that may be.

And you may incur legal costs to defend against such a pursuit. You also may have to pay something to rid yourself of a nuisance creditor only because it is the practical thing to do. "Success" then must be defined by asking where you would have been *without* the WealthSaver Trust. If you are no better for it, then the trust did *not* succeed. If you emerged the storm with *more* wealth intact than you otherwise would have, then it "succeeded." The WealthSaver Trust consistently exceeds this standard, and it does so more than any other asset protection strategy.

WEALTHSAVER HIGHLIGHTS

- No American with *any* wealth can afford to be without asset protection in these unsafe times.

- Protect your assets *before* you have legal problems. Later may be too late.

- The WealthSaver Trust can protect *any* asset against *any* creditor if properly constructed and timely funded.

- For the WealthSaver Trust to protect, the trust grantor cannot control the trust. Your assets entrusted to a professional trustee will be far safer than those you still control.

- The WealthSaver Trust can legally shelter your assets in bankruptcy, divorce and even from the IRS.

- The WealthSaver Trust is superior to domestic asset protection devices because it is not under the jurisdiction of U.S. courts. There is then less cause for concern over fraudulent transfer claims.

- Combining the WealthSaver Trust with the family limited partnership maximizes your ability to control *and* protect your assets.

- No other asset protection device shelters wealth as effectively as the WealthSaver Trust. Nothing has a better track record for creating lawsuit-proof, creditor-proof wealth!

3

FINDING PRIVACY IN A PUBLIC WORLD

The search for true financial secrecy and privacy is the second reason Americans expatriate their money offshore. They know that in today's America — and in most countries — personal and financial privacy no longer exists. What little we have we are rapidly losing. If you also believe it is your absolute right to keep your affairs completely confidential, you will find that this is only possible when your wealth is offshore. Only the offshore havens have secrecy laws. Only these havens believe that privacy is your inherent right — and a right to be absolutely protected! Privacy-seekers also realize that the WealthSaver Trust assures that your financial affairs will remain a tightly closed book.

Dr. Goldstein, why is financial privacy so important today?

You may not mind snoops probing your financial affairs. I know I do. So do other Americans who have turned to a WealthSaver Trust for confidentiality. They understand that only strict offshore secrecy laws can completely shield their financial affairs from an inquisitive IRS, creditors, competitors, ex-spouses and who-knows-who-else may be curious about their wealth. *Only* money sheltered in a WealthSaver Trust established in the *right* offshore haven fully privatizes *your* financial affairs, unlike the United States where your life and financial affairs are very public. You can never fully appreciate the WealthSaver Trust secrecy advantage *until* you suffer the indignity of some stranger or adversary rummaging through your financial and private records. Yet, this is everyday ritual in America and in most major countries where privacy is no longer respected.

Are more business people also seeking offshore privacy?

Many of my current clients are business people seeking privacy offshore. Secrecy is vital to *any* business that must protect valuable and sensitive financial and proprietary information from competitors, suppliers, customers and, of course, the government. Proprietary information is frequently a company's principal asset. Whatever the privacy motive, the offshore secrecy laws and WealthSaver Trust creates a confidentiality standard that can meet any secrecy need in our info-tech society.

Proprietary secrets (formulas, recipes, processes, plans) owned by your WealthSaver Trust can then be licensed to your U.S. company under a license agreement that requires strict confidentiality. All rights and possession of the data would instantly revert to the trust should the trade secrets in the possession of the U.S. company be subjected to subpoena or compulsory disclosure. In addition, the WealthSaver Trust will protect these trade secrets and proprietary rights from creditor claims and offer several interesting tax-saving possibilities.

Why hide information, unless it points to something illegal?

It is not only the crooks who want privacy. (But *even* the crooks deserve privacy!) I recall the insightful words of author Bill Petrocelli in his terrific book *Low Profile*: "The greatest degree of privacy in our society is achieved by the very rich, the very poor, and the very crooked."

I know *I* am neither very rich, very poor, nor very crooked, but, like most Americans, I strongly believe I am entitled to financial privacy. What I have earned, paid in taxes and scrimped to save is nobody's business. Does this simple search for privacy imply illegality? This presumption insults *every* American who shares my belief that his affairs should be his alone.

Those Americans with WealthSaver Trusts usually have specific and legitimate reasons for financial secrecy. It most often involves their business, competitors, taxes, relatives, litigation or estate planning. They are only ordinary, hardworking folks who merely want to mind their own business and have everyone else mind theirs!

How badly has our government eroded our financial privacy?

Uncle Sam did much more than erode our privacy. He obliterated it! Our government neither respects nor guarantees your privacy. Our laws force you to expose your every financial detail to *any* litigant, creditor, tax collector, ex-spouse, prospective heir, competitor, business associate or other curiosity seeker. National security and crime prevention are, of course, lame excuses Washington uses to poke more holes in your financial privacy. While our predatory society makes it critical to become financially invisible, our government makes it difficult, if not impossible. Of course, constitutional safeguards on privacy are a hoax.

Private records, even when incriminating, are not protected. Private records in your possession can be subpoenaed, as can your records entrusted to any American bank, investment broker, accountant, financial planner or anyone else — except your lawyer.

Study recent cases and you will see how easily your government can invade your personal or financial affairs. As a lawyer I am bewildered by this rapid erosion to our privacy. As an American, I am greatly saddened. But, I repeat, in our imperfect world why dwell on matters you cannot change? It's far smarter to secure secrecy offshore.

Where will it end? As the typical American, Uncle Sam now has about 25 active files on you and over 200 files if you are more visible or political. Washington's mammoth computers can instantly reveal whatever any oppressive government could possibly want to know about a citizen's finances, which it then freely shares with state and local officials and even private organizations that want to know more about *you*.

Your assets may *never* be threatened. You may *never* be sued. The government may *never* show a keen interest in you. But still you need confidentiality for countless personal reasons. Your investments can carry political overtones. Your past financial dealings can hurt your reputation or career. Visible wealth may attract swindlers, gold-diggers, ne'er-do-well family members, shady promoters and other parasites and vultures that populate our society? And because our own debt-ridden government wants a bigger bite of your wealth, it searches harder each year for more dollars to tax, more dollars to foolishly spend, and more dollars to confiscate from you and your family. Methodically dismantling our constitutional rights to privacy makes it all so possible.

How easily can someone discover our assets?

For $300 I can find out nearly everything about your finances. Between our high-powered computers and our vanished privacy rights, *anyone* can get a quick-fix on your wealth. The public records alone reveal mountains of information about you to private asset locators whose business it is to expose personal or business assets for plaintiffs' lawyers, creditors and our own government, in fact, anyone who will pay their small fee.

How secretive are our banking records?

We Americans are victimized by what we *don't* know.

Only the naive consider their bank *their* confidant, when in reality their bank is only a government informer.

Anyone can subpoena bank records. E*very* scrap of information your bank has on you or your finances is exposed. That's why more and more people won't entrust *their* financial records to a U.S. bank when only a few miles offshore are hundreds of banks that can and *must* keep their records secret.

Our Bank Secrecy Act certainly doesn't prevent unwarranted intrusions. The Bank Secrecy Act, contrary to its name, compels every American bank to record their customers' financial transactions. This law makes every banking transaction forever available to the government or any private party with a subpoena. This law compels your bank to microfilm or reproduce every check and draft drawn upon the bank or presented to it for payment, each check or draft received for deposit or collection, and the party for whom money was deposited or collected. Your bank must also report to the IRS your every cash transaction over $10,000, and if you rig your cash deposits or withdrawals to come under $10,000, you violate another "crime" called currency structuring. Big brother covered every escape route.

This law, probably more than any other, is what encourages so many Americans to bank offshore.

We will never reverse the trend until our government abandons their self-invoked right to monitor our finances.

Our privacy rights continue their decline. Uncle Sam spies more ingeniously than ever. The IRS is now perfecting a computer program that will force every commercial bank to screen over 800,000 daily electronic fund transfers for "suspicious" activity. The IRS is already wired to nearly every bank and most state and local agencies. Other agencies won't be outdone. Congress recently handed the FBI greatly expanded powers to seize records or wiretap phones without a warrant. These are the things that are happening in America *right now*, and that's why more people want their money out of America and into an offshore WealthSaver Trust. It's the surest way to slam the shutters on a government restrained by too few laws to stifle its growing curiosity.

How is financial secrecy achieved by the WealthSaver Trust?

The WealthSaver Trust cloaks your financial affairs under three impenetrable layers of secrecy. First, your trust will be established in a secrecy haven. This protects the confidentiality of *all* trust transactions. Second, the trust will conduct its business through a subsidiary International Business Corporation (IBC).

This will be formed in a separate secrecy haven that guarantees privacy for this entity. Third, the IBC will typically invest in still other secrecy havens, and your investment activities will thus be privatized. Someone must then pierce the rigid secrecy laws of at least three different secrecy havens to uncover your financial affairs. This, of course, is not likely.

Which havens are the best for "secrecy"?

The British Commonwealth havens offer good privacy for WealthSaver Trusts. Asset protection and privacy protection go hand in hand, so any WealthSaver Trust haven will feature reasonable privacy. The Cook Islands, Turks and Caicos, the Bahamas, the Cayman Islands, British Virgin Islands and Belize are other good secrecy havens; as are Nevis, Gibraltar and the Isle of Man.

Your trust funds may be invested in other excellent privacy havens. Liechtenstein, Switzerland, Austria or Luxembourg are good choices. You cannot establish WealthSaver Trusts in these havens, but they offer exceptional secrecy for funds invested by these trusts.

Finally, the IBC will typically be organized in the Bahamas, British Virgin Islands or Seychelles, which are also strong privacy havens. This is the triple privacy protection I refer to.

How strict are the offshore secrecy laws?

Offshore havens guarantee secrecy first through bank secrecy laws that protect *all* banking records against disclosure — whether to governments or private parties, and, second, through blocking statutes which prohibit the disclosure, copying, inspection or removal of documents, even under a foreign court order. This prevents the deposition or subpoena of witnesses within the haven.

You enjoy complete financial privacy with your money in a strong secrecy haven. They fully protect all bank records and transactions, including books, records and correspondence between yourself and your professional advisors, and also records of communications and transactions with common carriers. This same privacy extends to your agents, employees, directors, customers and all others in any way involved with your offshore finances.

These secrecy laws are very strictly obeyed because it is illegal for offshore banks to violate the secrecy laws, regardless of circumstances. Most havens harshly penalize secrecy-law violators and imprison errant bankers for ten or more years. The fact that offshore bankers who snitch on their depositors *go to jail* is a refreshing change from the U.S. where bankers go to jail for not snitching on their depositors. You also can sue your banker if he violates the haven's privacy laws.

For absolute privacy, you need the right haven, and the *right* haven is one without secrecy-destroying treaties with the U.S. In these havens, no government, no court and no legal process can compel disclosure. *Only* you as the depositor can waive your privacy rights.

Within these havens, you will find *true* privacy. Not qualified privacy. Not partial privacy. Not diminishing privacy. *This* is the privacy that is the bedrock for the financial freedom I speak about.

Why have some countries — such as Switzerland — become less secretive?

Secrecy can erode for several reasons: A secrecy haven may gradually prioritize other benefits, such as tax or asset protection, and then relax its privacy standards. Havens, like any other enterprise, also can become sloppy and lose their edge to new, more aggressive competitors who are anxious to attract more wealth and banking activity through tighter privacy laws. Whatever the reason, you must constantly guard against privacy erosion when you bank offshore. My firm constantly reviews offshore secrecy practices for clients mostly interested in strict secrecy. And we will quickly relocate a client's wealth if a haven no longer meets our strict privacy standards.

How seriously have recent treaties between the U.S. and a number of

secrecy havens compromised their privacy?

Several offshore secrecy havens have succumbed to U.S. economic, legal or political pressures to relax their privacy. These countries relied heavily on U.S. financial support, and such countries are always a poor choice when privacy is your objective. However, you must objectively evaluate the actual impact of these treaties on privacy.

Switzerland, for example, drops its secrecy veil *only* under circumstances carefully prescribed in their treaty with the United States. American prosecutors can only obtain financial information from the Swiss when there is ample evidence of a crime recognized under Swiss law. Fortunately for many Americans, this does *not* include tax evasion. U.S. depositors also can petition the Swiss government not to reveal financial information, and many such appeals are decided on behalf of the depositor. Swiss banking secrecy remains relatively airtight without clear evidence of such crimes as drug trafficking or money laundering that are also crimes in Switzerland.

Other "secrecy" havens are *less* secretive. Secrecy is comparative. You must constantly compare secrecy standards, particularly in our fast-moving world where laws, treaties and international relationships change so quickly. Havens bound to U.S. tax treaties must specify precisely the circumstances and the cooperation level under which the haven will release information to the United States in uncovering offshore financial transactions.

I have concern over the long-term effects of the Mutual Legal Assistance Treaties (MLATs). These treaties now primarily target individuals engaged in non-tax related crimes, but these laws will eventually become a lever for the United States to extract more and more information concerning any American's offshore finances and regardless of purpose. I avoid MLAT havens for WealthSaver Trusts, but I may eventually run out of such havens. The United States is an overgrown political octopus that stretches its tentacles of influence to nearly every country. And few can resist. Our future challenge will be to find that rare haven that refuses to go to bed with Uncle Sam.

In practice, how do offshore banks insure secrecy to their American depositors?

First, understand how American banks operate. If you are an American involved in a lawsuit or dispute with the government, your American bank must then give your opponent any bank records they may subpoena. Your offshore records, on the other hand, would be fully protected from these same U.S. court orders and subpoenas because your offshore bank *cannot* legally divulge financial information about you to *anyone*, unless there are treaty provisions to the contrary.

Offshore banks are also jurisdictionally immune to service of process. This is important because it effectively bars writs of execution or attachment orders. Secrecy laws in most havens not only protect entrusted funds from creditor seizure on a domestic judgment, but these same laws also protect the confidentiality of every banking transaction. Under no circumstances, whether it is a civil lawsuit or criminal investigations, will an offshore bank disclose protected information.

If your offshore bank has no presence in the U.S., through American-based branches or affiliates, it will be beyond the jurisdiction of American courts. Information demands also will be barred by our American courts if such disclosure would violate the secrecy laws of the offshore haven. This is true even if the offshore bank is owned or operated by U.S. residents because the offshore bank is considered a separate entity obligated to protect the confidentiality of *all* depositors. The secrecy laws of every country prohibit using a bank principal's citizenry to circumvent the privacy laws that extend to the offshore bank.

The net effect then is that all requests for bank information, whether through legal process or otherwise, will be rejected or ignored by the bank. No records will be produced. No bank employee will testify. No representative involved with your finances within the haven will be questioned. And no government agency or private litigant can compel otherwise.

Dr. Goldstein, at one of your recent WealthSaver seminars you commented that to insure privacy you must separate your offshore finances from your U.S. finances. Can you please expand upon that?

You gain maximum offshore financial privacy by creating two entirely separate financial worlds. Your *public* world is your home country. This is where you work, pay taxes, keep your bank accounts and other investments and financial matters that you expect the world to know about.

Your *private* world is offshore. That's where you keep your "invisible" money: funds and other investments that only you, close family members and your offshore professionals know about. This private world keeps your major bank accounts, investments, business interests and other nest egg assets invisible.

For absolute secrecy you must keep your private and public worlds separate. You achieve this by avoiding direct transactions between the two, such as direct transfers between your onshore (public world) bank and offshore (private world) bank. Secrecy is always compromised when expatriated money is too easily traced. To increase privacy, you must indirectly transfer your funds through one or more intermediaries, using an offshore company for redeposit to your offshore account is one example.

There is no need to maintain privacy between offshore accounts. Once money is deposited to one offshore haven, an investigator cannot discover other offshore accounts through transfers between these accounts — if both offshore accounts are secretive. You sacrifice privacy *only* when one haven is less secretive. To secretly repatriate funds, you would reverse the process and re-channel funds to the United States through offshore intermediaries.

Are there other ways to quietly move your money offshore into a WealthSaver Trust?

Most people with WealthSaver Trusts *don't* try to conceal the transfer of their funds to the trust. They only want their finances kept secret once they're offshore. Those who don't fully understand how the WealthSaver Trust protects assets consider it important to secretly transfer their funds offshore because they mistakenly believe secrecy provides the asset protection. Of course, this is untrue. The trust's provisions and the haven's trust laws together protect the funds. WealthSaver Trust assets are no less protected because an American creditor knows about the trust. However, many people still insist upon secretly diverting their funds offshore. This, of course, is futile because you cannot conceal either the asset transfer or the trust if a creditor compels you to disclose these matters under oath.

The U.S. mail is the most common way to transfer funds offshore. You can legally send a check or money order for any amount to any offshore haven, and this method is generally the most convenient. With a few additional tricks you can maximize privacy. First, never use a personal check, even for small amounts. The Bank Privacy Act will require your bank to record every check you write above $10,000; however, most banks microfilm *all* checks. Wire transfers over $3,000 are also recorded. *Nearly all* offshore banks wire transfer funds to correspondent banks or foreign exchange dealers in the United States. Speed is the advantage and a wire transfer can usually be completed within 48 hours. It's preferable to wire money market funds to your offshore bank and have the funds identified only by account number and accompanied by a letter of instruction.

Another possibility is to buy bonds under $10,000, as these would not be reportable to customs. One bond mailed each day can quickly build a tidy offshore nest egg. To avoid a paper trail, you would pay cash for the bonds. You can also mail cash in amounts up to $10,000. This obviously is not the smartest way to transfer funds; however, people do mail cash offshore with surprisingly few losses.

Money orders and cashier's checks are also two excellent ways to mail funds offshore. Money orders over $10,000 must be payable to a specific offshore bank or some other payee. Since it is not "bearer" currency, it is not reportable to Customs. Money orders over $10,000 payable to "cash" are bearer currency and, like cash, are reportable to Customs. Money orders under $10,000 paid to "cash" are not reportable if you mail only one money order at a time. However, you must observe the currency structuring laws and be guided by your lawyer so you don't inadvertently violate them. For maximum secrecy, you may eliminate your name from the money order. An accompanying side letter, can instruct the bank to deposit the funds to your account.

Cashier's checks can be purchased with cash for transferring larger amounts offshore. This is still another way to break the paper trail. Your check will bear only the bank manager's signature and will be untraceable to you. As with money orders, cashier's checks above $10,000 must be payable to a specific payee (such as your offshore bank or company) and not "cash" if you are to avoid Customs reporting.

International transactions chiefly involve only intangible computer entries via telephone, telex or tele-copier. So it is remarkably easy to bank offshore with advance planning, thanks to modern electronics. And you can do so with considerable privacy.

Another way to transfer funds offshore unde-tected is to send a third-party check made out to yourself. The cancelled check will not be returned to your account but to that third party's bank, and create only another invisible paper trail.

The simplest way to send money offshore secretly? Transfer it via your attorney's trust account. Attorney records are privileged unless the attorney is involved with a client in a fraudulent scheme. Even then it will be difficult to access your attorney's finan-cial records. There are, nevertheless, few instances when a diligent creditor or the IRS cannot discover the transfer of large sums of money from the United States to an offshore account.

How practical is it to personally carry money offshore?

Personally transporting money offshore is both expen-sive and inconvenient. But it is an alternative, and perhaps a good one if your haven can double as a vacation spot. You must remember that $10,000 or more per person transferred offshore in cash, travelers checks or other bearer currency must be reported to U.S. Customs. Customs can disclose this to the IRS and other federal agencies but will not disclose this transfer to private parties.

Many people prefer to personally transport such precious commodities as diamonds, rare coins or gold. Once offshore, these can easily be converted to funds for deposit. Their advantage is that commodities are not reportable to Customs, regardless of value. You must never evade Customs reporting. The penalty can be 20 years in jail and forfeiture of the assets.

For confidentiality, would you follow similar procedures to repatriate your money?

You also can repatriate up to $10,000 in cash or bearer currency without notifying Customs. This is again practical *if* you frequently visit your haven. Or your offshore bank can wire your funds to you at a domestic bank through "pay by identification." You need only identify yourself to the correspondent U.S. bank to retrieve your money. This transfer *will* destroy secrecy because it directly links your two financial worlds. It is therefore preferable to wire transfer the funds through intermediary accounts.

You may find the most convenient way to repatriate your funds is to have your offshore bank send you frequent bank drafts on the account of its American correspondent banks. Every offshore bank has one or more correspondent banks in major U.S. cities.

Another strategy is to have your offshore bank give you a Visa credit card for use within the United States. Since these transactions will be cleared in the offshore haven and not the U.S., you can spend down your offshore funds with reasonable privacy.

What information concerning the offshore WealthSaver Trust should be held confidential?

If you have creditors, your objective *may* be to secure complete confidentiality. You would then not voluntarily disclose:

1. The existence of the trust or any ancillary entities, such as the IBC.

2. The trust terms.

3. The name of any grantor, beneficiary, trustee, protector, investment advisor or custodian.

4. The amount initially or subsequently transferred to the trust.

5. The trust assets or their location.

6. Where the trust is established.

7. Where the IBC is established.

It may, as a tactical matter, be smarter to let a creditor know about the trust (but not the other points) for purposes of either discouraging litigation or facilitating an advantageous settlement. This, of course, must be decided on a case-by-case basis and is a strategic issue best left to your attorney.

It is important to be circumspect in matters concerning your WealthSaver Trust and not to talk about it to those who are not directly involved with it. You must expect the same confidentiality from your U.S. accountant, attorney and financial planner.

You need not concern yourself about confidentiality with your foreign trustees and protectors. As with offshore banks, many countries also impose secrecy on their trustees and other fiduciaries. Confidentiality is rigidly observed as a matter of custom in all other WealthSaver Trust havens.

Can an American creditor force you to disclose your offshore finances under a court order?

Yes. And you must then truthfully disclose all matters concerning the trust that *you know about*. This would include disclosing the funds you transferred offshore, their source and the *known* trust investments. However, when you have creditor problems, your trustee will ordinarily switch into new investments that you *do not know about*. This insures that through your trustee a creditor cannot discover your *present* trust assets. However, this is only an added precaution. A creditor has little recourse even when he does know about your trust investments.

Won't tax returns disclose your offshore finances?

As a grantor of a WealthSaver Trust, you must pay taxes on income earned by the trust. However, you will not disclose on the tax return those trust assets that produced that income. It is nearly impossible to discover specific trust assets through a tax return. Moreover, records with foreign trustees cannot be obtained. A creditor can, however, subpoena a U.S. protector, who would logically have knowledge of your trust assets. This is why you should use *only* foreign protectors as well as foreign trustees when you have creditors investigating the trust.

There are other IRS reporting requirements in addition to your 1040 income tax return, and we will talk about them later. But reporting isn't always required. Reporting depends on the type of

WealthSaver Trust. More importantly, reporting to the IRS provides only the narrowest glimpse of your off-shore finances.

The IRS is now urging Congress to tighten the reporting requirements for WealthSaver Trusts. I antic-ipate these laws will pass and that there will soon be considerably more reporting with these trusts. You must stay abreast of these changing reporting require-ments so that you do not unintentionally violate them.

Must WealthSaver Trust grantors comply with the banking disclosure law that compels U.S. citizens with foreign bank accounts which total or exceed $10,000 in any tax year to report these annually to the government?

Grantors of WealthSaver Trusts *may* be exempt from reporting *if* they have no signing authority or control over the WealthSaver Trust account or no interest as a beneficiary. Any American with signing authority — even trustees and protectors — must check this box notwithstanding that they have no beneficial or direct financial interest in the trust. I advise my WealthSaver Trust clients to check the box in all circumstances. There's no danger in acknowledging an account because disclosure does not increase the probability of an audit.

Forms that are filed with the Treasury

Department are non-IRS forms and are not considered tax information. Therefore, this information is *not* subject to the IRS Code restrictions that limit disclosure of return information.

IRS and Treasury Department reporting requirements can be complex and may or may not apply to your WealthSaver Trust. For that reason you must review your requirements at least annually with your attorney and/or tax advisor who may also apprise you of the more recent reporting requirements.

Is a beneficiary entitled to information concerning the trust?

Quite frequently a grantor will prefer that certain beneficiaries — such as his children — not know about the trust. The grantor may believe the children will work harder or be less demanding if unaware of their future inheritance. In other cases, confidentiality is desired to discourage claims by a beneficiary's spouse under a divorce or from other creditors of the beneficiary.

Nevertheless, a beneficiary, either by the trust terms or applicable law of the trust haven, *does* have the right to information concerning the trust. At the least, this would include the basic trust terms, the trust assets, the trustee's activities and the identification of other parties to the trust, including other beneficiaries.

A grantor must guard against advising a beneficiary of his or her interest in the trust — or even that a trust exists. This may be the only way to avoid an inquiry from a beneficiary. Because beneficiaries are normally discretionary, the trustee could probably argue with success that he does not recognize the individual as a beneficiary and therefore that individual is not entitled to the demanded information since he is *not* a beneficiary. Creditors, or others with an interest adverse to the beneficiary, are in no better position than the beneficiary when it comes to obtaining information concerning the trust.

Which offshore banks are most secretive?

I prefer Liechtenstein bank accounts for secrecy. Austria was once good, but its secrecy was weakened by its recent treaties with the United States. Bahamian and Cayman banks are still reasonably good for secrecy, as are banks in Gibraltar, Cyprus, the Isle of Man and Channel Islands. The *most* secretive bank account is the Hong Kong chop account. No name appears on the account and all transactions involve only complex Chinese symbols.

Gold and other collectibles, of course, leave no paper trail, and collectibles in a safe deposit box is most private. But keep in mind, your offshore WealthSaver accounts will *never be* in your name. It is

Asset Protection   1/24/98

1. All assets
2. Against all creditors
3. With certainty.

Homestead, Retirement Acc'ts,
IRA's, Life Ins., Stock ("S")
Past Assets — Conveyances
Future Assets — Inheritances
Tangible, Intangible (Copyrights, Royalties)

Creditors have rights!
Law of <u>fradulent</u> <u>transfer</u> (Conveyance)
against a <u>present</u> creditor for
less than fair value with the
effect of cheating the creditor.

unlikely *anyone* can connect you to the account except through your own disclosure.

Wouldn't the recorded trust document itself reveal confidential information?

Most trust jurisdictions do *not* require that you file the entire trust. For instance, Nevis records *only* the trust name and then issues a certificate of registration to the trustee. The trust document itself is not recorded or public record. This keeps confidential the beneficiaries, the grantor, the trustees, the protector and the terms of the trust. Unless the grantor retains a copy of these trust documents within the United States, it will be impossible for a creditor to obtain them from your foreign trustee or protector.

WEALTHSAVER HIGHLIGHTS

- Privacy is extinct in the United States and in most major countries. For privacy you *must* go offshore!

- WealthSaver Trust havens are also excellent secrecy havens. They privatize all banking and financial affairs, and a breach of secrecy is a most serious crime in these WealthSaver Trust havens.

- The WealthSaver Trust guarantees privacy three

ways: 1) through the secrecy laws where the trust is established, 2) the secrecy laws of the haven where the trust's subsidiary corporation is established, and 3) the secrecy laws where the trust funds are invested.

- To maximize privacy, you should keep your onshore finances separate from your offshore finances.

- Your trust *is* not usually public record. Trust matters are then only between you, your protector and your trustee.

- The WealthSaver Trust can be your path to maximum privacy if you prize privacy!

WEALTH BUILDING WITH YOUR WEALTHSAVER TRUST

*T*he WealthSaver Trust not only protects *wealth; it also builds wealth. Your WealthSaver Trust can be your passport to an entirely new and huge constellation of more profitable investment opportunities in a truly global economy.*

International investing is exciting. Rewarding. Fast-paced. The story is always the same: Offshore securities and mutual funds consistently outperform comparable U.S. investments. You can trade Eurodollars and other foreign currencies which consistently outperform the American dollar on the international exchanges. Dynamic trends in international investing consistently occur elsewhere — outside the United States!

Wherever, however and whatever you invest, the WealthSaver Trust is your best vehicle through which to invest. Securing offshore investments in a WealthSaver Trust will provide you maximum protection, privacy and profits.

Considering the many high-quality American investments, why should Americans invest elsewhere?

One word: diversification. Smart investors *diversify*. And you cannot diversify only by company or industry. You must also diversify geographically. You cannot afford to put all your investment eggs in one basket. Nobody can.

When you invest globally you no longer bet your entire nest egg on the economic or political stability of any one country. You spread your risk. Still, people fail to heed the lessons of history. From every corner of the globe are citizens of other lands who forfeited their wealth either through confiscation or economic erosion. Who can say it won't happen in the United States?

If you are one of the millions of Americans who still believes offshore investing is too risky, you must open your eyes. Statistics prove you *reduce* your investment risk when you invest globally. You *increase* your risk when you confine yourself only to American investments.

Offshore investing also brings opportunity. Through international investing, you can take advantage of any company or any market in the world. Only myopic isolationists believe *all* the best deals are here in America. At current stock market levels, we can only conclude that most of the best global investments are *elsewhere*. To get ahead financially, you must capitalize on the booming global markets. It will not only be a more certain way to accumulate wealth in the decade ahead, but it will also be the most certain way to keep it.

Will more global investing by Americans force Washington to restrict or ban foreign investing?

It is inevitable. The question is *when*. Since our founding, we Americans could legally expatriate our money. But the doors will close when too many Americans lose confidence in our economy and too much "flight-capital" leaves our country. As historically happened elsewhere, our government will then force you to keep your money right here in the United States. Then it will be too late to expatriate your money to foreign lands that promise greater financial safety and prosperity. When that happens — as it will — you will then lose one more precious freedom: the right to protect, invest and spend your money *where* and *how you want!*

How soon will this happen? Very soon! Washington is even now constricting our ability to invest offshore through more burdensome reporting requirements; closing the few remaining offshore tax loopholes; and by imposing new taxes and economic sanctions on Americans who invest internationally. Congress has not yet outlawed currency expatriation, but it is unquestionably trying to make it less attractive.

That's why I confidently predict severe or even total foreign exchange controls by the end of the century. The explosion in WealthSaver Trusts is at least partly due to this fear that next year may be too late to expatriate your money.

America was traditionally the #1 financial center, so isn't the offshore megatrend a surprising reversal of our fortunes?

Why should the offshore megatrend be surprising? Congress itself made the strongest case for Americans to invest offshore in its own staff report:

"... The offshore financial market has many advantages for rational economic operations. The Euromarket efficiently serves national governments, semi-public agencies, private corporations and individuals. The reasonable expectation, when one learns that an entity is engaged offshore, is that it is there for honest economic reasons, buttressed by whatever advantages privacy holds. The major categories for offshore use are to profit from higher interest rates when lending, to enjoy lower interest rates when borrowing, to escape taxation, to enjoy greater business flexibility by avoiding regulation in an efficient market, to enjoy the protection of confidentiality when engaged in activities, which if known to others in advance might hazard business success or profit margins, and, through the confidentiality mechanisms, to hedge and enjoy other risk-allaying methods through offshore diversification, liquidity, forward speculations and the like."

This objective message from Washington is one *every* American must listen to!

You sound pessimistic about the U.S. economy. How does our economy compare to others?

I love America, and I believe America has a great future. But I also say we *are* heading for very tough times economically. Over the next decade or two it will be financially hazardous and probably disastrous to hold your *entire* wealth in U.S. dollars. The warnings are everywhere:

- Twenty years ago the United States controlled over half the world's total economy. We now control less than one-third. By 2000 we will control only one-sixth the global economy.

- In the same two decades, our U.S. dollar lost at least half its value against several stronger currencies, In the next five years, the U.S. dollar will lose value even faster and against many more currencies.

- America was once the world's leading industrial power but now trails in most major industries.

- The U.S. is no longer the world's banker. We are a debtor nation. Our trade balance is perilous. Our national debt defies mathematical measure and grows daily. Our financial trends are frightening.

And as our debt grows, so will our taxes, inflation, economic instability and social unrest. The most patriotic American will be forced offshore with his money.

As we approach the millennium, you must no longer consider yourself *only* an American citizen. You are a citizen of a vast international marketplace — a marketplace where you as an American will have much less spending and earning power. Devalued wealth held hostage in America will make you considerably poorer.

Is the declining U.S. dollar a reason for global investing?

Yes, but only because a declining U.S. dollar most rapidly destroys your spending power. Financially savvy Americans realize that the *only* way to survive the declining U.S. dollar's wealth-robbing effect is to trade in *stronger* foreign currencies.

You must invest in strong overseas currencies to more clearly see the U.S. dollar's erratic fluctuations. Foreign currencies that rise against the U.S. dollar can, of course, be converted into more U.S. dollars which you can then spend or invest at home. Any change in the U.S. dollar's value automatically re-values your foreign-based investments. An eroding U.S. dollar is always painful when you are solely invested in the United States. It is far less painful when you diversify into foreign currencies.

Are WealthSaver Trust investments usually denominated in U.S. dollars or foreign currency?

As the grantor you can recommend to the trustee the currency denomination for your investment. Most offshore investments can be denominated either in U.S. currency or foreign currency. Considering the offshore currency opportunities, most Americans switch out of the U.S. dollar and into the yen, mark, Swiss franc or even the peso. If your judgment is good and your timing right, you can earn exceptional profits trading outside the U.S. dollar. Currency futures are another superb way to diversify your stock and bond portfolio. Probably 80 percent of my clients invest in foreign currencies. I particularly recommend the Swiss franc. I am convinced it will consistently outperform the U.S. dollar by a wide margin over the next several years.

What percentage of your net worth should you invest offshore?

If your primary goal is asset protection, then you would invest as much as possible. If asset protection is not your immediate goal, you would probably invest only your nest egg or that portion of your wealth you reserved for your retirement and that you do not presently need for your support.

Only a decade or so ago, financial advisors counseled their more wealthy American clients to internationally invest about 20 percent of their money. Today's advisors now earmark 60 percent, or more, for foreign investments. But you should not completely abandon your U.S. investments. A significant and immediate portfolio shift toward more offshore investments is a good start.

What are the pointers to intelligently start an offshore investment program?

To intelligently invest offshore, you must follow the common-sense rules for investing *anywhere*:

1. Learn everything you can about offshore investments before you invest. Read the numerous offshore financial journals. Study the prospectus on every offshore financial product that interests you. There's no substitute for knowledge.

2. Decide how much you will initially invest offshore once you decide how much you can invest *anywhere*.

3. Retain a good offshore financial advisor who knows the U.S. tax laws. If your trustee recommends investments, then obtain the opinion of an independent advisor. Foreign trustees earn commissions by selling financial products. They *may* be excellent investments, but you need impartial guidance.

4. Select only *safe* offshore investments. Financial products from Caribbean and other third-world havens are too risky. European investments are the safest.

5. Choose offshore investments customized to

your financial objectives. And it is easier to customize with offshore investments because they are more varied than American investments.

6. Diversify. Never put all your eggs in one offshore basket. Select many different investments in many countries.

7. Invest cautiously. Don't jump too fast into offshore investing. Test your investments. Test your advisors. Are you comfortable with your investments? Invest more only when you have a solid offshore investment program.

How are Investments selected for the WealthSaver trust?

The WealthSaver trustee must legally select all investments, but the trustee will usually follow your investment requests *if* your investment preferences are prudent and lawful. Offshore trustees work closely with trust grantors to shape the investment portfolios that the grantors want. Other trustees may rely upon independent investment advisors or asset managers for investment recommendations or even leave investment decisions to the advisor. An independent investment advisor will cost, but the right advisor can also be an excellent investment.

Because the trustee has the complete discretion to invest, the trustee must exhibit a superior investment record. Your trustee also must understand your investment objectives, the investments appropriate for your goals, and the investments with which you will be most comfortable.

Do not attempt to usurp the trustee's right to select the investments. The trustee must have the legal authority over investment decisions subject only to protector approval. That is how it must be. If the grantor controls the trust investments, an American court can conclude that the grantor also has sufficient control to repatriate the funds to satisfy creditor claims. The WealthSaver Trust would then provide no asset protection. In practice, your trustee *will* follow your prudent investment preferences if you are not under duress (court compulsion).

How do you select a good foreign investment advisor for the trust?

You can find excellent investment advisors in every haven. I work with several foreign investment advisors or asset management firms, and they have accomplished significant results for my clients.

An excellent choice is Lines Overseas Management (Cayman) Ltd., in Grand Cayman. LOMC is the most established offshore brokerage house, managing a significant amount of money for many of the world's wealthiest individuals. LOMC carries fraud, theft, errors and omissions insurance for $5 million to ensure the safety of your assets.

LOMC has an enviable track record with private placements, offering the same range of products and services that you would expect from a domestic brokerage firm but also introducing a fresh global outlook toward your investment strategy. You will receive prompt execution of your trades and professional service. Call Scott Oliver, offshore asset manager, at (809) 949-5808.

One of the drawbacks to dealing with an offshore investment advisor is the time and distance equation. Oftentimes your advisor is leaving the office just as you are getting to yours. I have found a U.S. firm, Global Assets Advisors (GAA) to have a solid reputation based upon knowledge and expertise in the international markets. The firm is a wholly owned subsidiary of International Assets Holding Corporation, a NASDAQ-listed financial services company that focuses on international investments headquartered in Winter Park, Florida.

GAA serves as the capital management arm of the group and can manage funds located anywhere in the world. Thus if you set up an offshore trust, GAA could be retained as investment advisor to that entity and manage the investment of your funds into Switzerland, Japan, Hong Kong or even back into the

United States, using whichever offshore brokerage firm or bank you designate. This arrangement allows you to separate the functions of custodian and advisor, providing a system of checks and balances. A sister company of GAA, a broker/dealer called International Assets, publishes a monthly newsletter on foreign investments and a free trial subscription can be obtained by calling (800) 432-0000 and mentioning this book.

Also consider the Nassau-based Security Traders International Limited. This discount broker holds its clients' assets securely in segregated numbered accounts with an international trading subsidiary of the Hong Kong and Shanghai Banking Corporation, one of the largest and strongest banks in the world. Beneficial ownership is disclosed to no one. They can be reached at (809) 356-3237 voice and 356-6144 fax or at www.investoffshore.com on Internet."

The offshore organizations as well as offshore publications advertise the names of foreign investment advisors. Offshore Investment (+44-417-122-505-50) is probably the best resource. Offshore trust companies and banks usually have good investment departments. Their fees compare favorably to investment advisors in the United States. Your trustee should have a few investment advisors or asset management firms to suggest.

Scrutinize any perspective advisor carefully. It is clear that you cannot rely upon their marketing materials alone. Approach the selection process by asking seven questions about a prospective advisor:

1. Does the firm specialize in the type and range of investments that interest you?

2. Does the firm's investment policy parallel your own?

3. Does the firm have a significant number of clients similar to you?

4. Does the firm have the personnel and organization to deliver quality service?

5. Does the firm provide the range of services you require or that are provided by competitive firms?

6. Does the firm charge competitive fees?

7. Does the firm have a good track record — particularly with comparable clients with similar portfolios?

Why not be your own investment advisor? Probably the one best source for offshore investment information is through the Investors Alliance at 219 Commercial Blvd., Ft. Lauderdale, FL 33339. The Investors Alliance has available for its members numerous resources for better investing both domestically and offhsore. They can provide you all the information you will need to become an intelligent global investor. Readers who own a computer and want an excellent source of information can obtain a computer CD-ROM with detailed information on thousands of companies worldwide, including many foreign investments which trade as American Depository Receipts for $89 from the Investors Alliance. *(See Appendix)*

Does the investment advisor have the discretion to make investment decisions on his own?

That is permitted in some contracts and other contracts leave the investment decisions solely to the trustee. Non-discretionary contracts are probably the exception rather than the rule.

Nearly all advisory contracts can be terminated on short notice, so there is always an opportunity to change advisors if their advisory performance does not meet expectations.

How safe are foreign custodial banks that hold the WealthSaver Trust funds?

The 122 largest and wealthiest banks are *all* offshore. Banks naturally thrive more in an offshore environment that is specifically designed to attract depositor money.

Offshore banking caters to today's sophisticated, well-heeled customer who demands higher-level banking services. And you cannot question the stability of such offshore banking giants as Swiss Bank Corporation and Union Bank of Switzerland, or the United Kingdom's Barclays, Westminster or Royal Bank of Scotland. There are banking giants everywhere.

Even the smaller havens have top rate banks, but they are also dotted with private banks that never advertise for deposits, never publish financial statements and are only brass-plated names on doors. Offshore banks are also regulated. Switzerland's banking regulations are in many ways more rigid than our own. Smaller havens less regulate their banks. This accounts for hundreds of shaky private banks and depositor anxiety in dealing with these banks.

Offshore banking has negligible risk *if* you stay with the larger, more well-established banks. Foreign banks fail less frequently than American banks; however, because you have no depositor insurance, only a financially sound bank can give you comfort that your money is safe.

Your trustee must *carefully* choose a bank for the trust. A trustee is liable if he negligently selects a weak bank that later fails. Foreign trustees in that regard are usually quite diligent and cautious.

Which country has the strongest banking system?

For convenience, trustees normally bank in their own country. However, a WealthSaver Trust custodian bank can be anywhere in the world, provided it is *outside* the U.S.

For asset protection, you would select a haven without treaties or comity arrangements that would allow American creditors ready access to the funds. For example, Isle of Man or Channel Islands banks are appreciably safer than United Kingdom banks for this purpose. Privacy is another factor. Again, a trust's custodial account should be located in a haven with strict secrecy laws.

There's no one answer as to which haven is best for banking because the havens offer different banking features. Do you mostly prize privacy, asset protection, higher interest, convenience, or low or no taxes?

Liechtenstein, Luxembourg, Hungary, Cook Islands, Nevis, Belize, Cayman Islands and Bahamaian banks are my favorites for privacy. Switzerland is also still good. Most American accounts are in these havens. Their interest rates compare to ours, but are generally below Pacific Rim rates.

Isle of Man banks consistently pay the highest interest. Their security is also good. Privacy in the Isle of Man is not as secure as in many other havens, but it is more than adequate. These banks are easily reached from England.

WealthSaver havens with tax-free banking include the Bahamas, Caymans, Turks and Caicos Islands, Vanuatu, Bermuda, British Virgin Islands and Monserrat. Most others are low-tax havens.

Our office maintains a current list of rated offshore banks that we will gladly make available upon request.

How do interest rates from offshore banks compare to U.S. banks?

Offshore bank accounts average about two points higher than U.S. bank interest rates. But you must shop to get these rates.

Much of the American capital is invested in foreign banks because their interest approximates yields available only from higher-risk American securities. The net consequence is that *trillions* of American dollars have departed American banks for the more generous Bahamian, Cayman, Austrian or Swiss banks.

What services should a custodian bank provide?

Offshore custodian banks offer about the same services you would expect from your U.S. bank and several others besides:

- Cash cards and credit cards.

- Cash deposits.

- Correspondent banks in principal countries and cities.

- Fast and easy deposits, withdrawals and money transfers.

- SWIFT memberships.

- Mail-holds for depositors.

- Instructions by phone, fax or mail.

A custodial bank's most important service is fast, easy withdrawals. Some foreign banks make withdrawals a difficult ritual, demanding notarized letters of instruction, endless forms and imposing bureaucratic delays that can lengthen the withdrawal process. Banks that accept faxed withdrawal instructions and secret code word authentications provide the fastest withdrawals. Quick withdrawals are essential to hasten the transfer of funds for asset protection when the trust is under creditor attack.

Another important banking convenience is the "all-in-one" account. This will offer:

- Single and multiple currency checks, including the popular Eurochecks.

- Global credit and debit cards (PLUS and Visa).

- Simplified transfers between savings and checking accounts.

- Interest tied to money market rates.

- Credit cards in various currencies.

No custodian bank will offer every service, so you should select a custodian bank that features those services that are most important to you.

Banking fees range considerably. To attract depositors, the offshore banks, particularly Caribbean banks, often dangle no-charge banking. This, however, can be the *most* expensive because of many hidden costs. A bank must always recoup its expenses, whether it is through lower interest, rigid penalties for violating the bank's always numerous banking rules, temporary fee reductions or hiked fee waivers. Offshore banks with no activity charges or no/low balance charges are usually the most costly overall.

What accounts do foreign custodian banks offer?

Foreign banks feature several different account options:

- *Deposit accounts* compare to U.S. savings accounts, except that they impose more withdrawal restrictions. Offshore banks require advance notice of intended withdrawals above a set amount.

- *Current accounts* compare to U.S. checking accounts. Many offshore banks do not issue checkbooks, which is unimportant because you would not pay everyday bills from your trust.

- *Savings accounts* pay higher interest than deposit accounts; however, they also have stricter withdrawal requirements.

- *Investment savings* accounts pay higher interest than savings accounts and also have stricter withdrawal requirements.

- *Custodial accounts* are offshore safe deposit boxes.

- *Cash bonds* compare to U.S. certificates of deposit. They commit your funds to the bank for a minimum time period with early withdrawal penalties.

- *Eurocurrency accounts* allow you to trade in other foreign currencies if the bank acts as your broker.

Besides difference in account features and titles, offshore and U.S. bank accounts also differ in their primary function: Offshore banks chiefly sell privacy and secrecy. This is not the hallmark of American banks. American banks are primarily lenders. Offshore banks prefer to attract capital and to invest.

What credit cards are available from offshore custodian banks?

Offshore "plastic" is available in the form of a cash card, a debit card or a combination card. Usually they are marketed offshore under different names. The cash card allows you to withdraw cash from an automated teller machine. It protects privacy because it leaves a minimum paper trail. Cash cards are international, allowing you to access cash in hundreds of countries. Major credit cards include PLUS cash cards (the largest), ETC cash cards (Far East) and Visa (everywhere).

The debit card is a substitute for our U.S. checking account but is more convenient. The debit card, like a credit card, only debits your account. The bank does not extend you credit, which avoids the paper trail from credit transactions.

Virtually every offshore bank issues credit cards, although most are limited to the debit cards that require a compensating balance about twice your outstanding credit balance.

The more progressive custodian banks also issue combination cards. These are the most valuable cards because they merge the functions and benefits of cash, credit and debit cards and also can be used for check guarantees.

How is a foreign custodian account opened?

An offshore bank account can be opened in person or by mail. Swiss banks require a personal interview. Visiting the bank is recommended if it will also build your own confidence with an unfamiliar bank.

Your trustee will open the custodian account for the trust and its International Business Corporation as well. You should have no more involvement than to send a check or wire transfer funds from your U.S. bank to your trustee or trust account on the instructions of a trustee. You may also have to send your trustee your photo ID and reference letters for transmittal to the bank. Offshore banks do want to know who they are doing business with and avoid suspicious depositors.

What is the working relationship between the foreign trustee, investment advisor and custodian bank?

If the investment advisor has complete investment discretion, he will communicate all trades with the custodian who will execute and confirm these trades. Where the trustee retains the control over investments, the trades will be undertaken on the *advice* of the investment advisor. Of course, these three functions may be merged in one or two parties rather than three separate parties.

The trustee has the overall responsibility for the proper execution of the investment program and therefore must be attentive to whether the investment advisor and custodial bank are properly performing.

What investment functions can the grantor or beneficiaries perform?

Neither the grantor nor a beneficiary can assert any control over the trust administration, and that will include its investment policies. For example, the grantor and beneficiaries should avoid:

1. Sending funds to the custodian. (All funds should be sent directly to the trustee.)

2. Any direct contact with the custodian or investment advisor. All contact must be through the trustee or protector.

3. Selecting the investment advisor or custodian. The grantor may interview prospective advisors and custodians and make

recommendations; however, the trustee must in all instances have the full and final authority for managing the trust, including all aspects of the investment program.

If a creditor can prove that a grantor or beneficiary directly and regularly communicates with an investment advisor or custodian, or otherwise controls their actions or the investment program, then a court may conclude the trust is only a sham and set it aside.

The grantor *should* and the beneficiaries *may* receive periodic reports from the trustee to reflect the status of the trust's investments. However, the right to an accounting from the custodian or investment advisor must remain with the trustee.

Which offshore investments are most popular for WealthSaver Trusts?

My own clients mostly prefer commercial annuities (mutual funds wrapped by insurance) because they are safe and also tax-deferred. International mutual funds rank second in popularity. Very few Americans invest directly in offshore stocks or bonds as foreign securities are usually purchased indirectly through mutual funds. Collectibles — precious metals (gold, silver, platinum) — are also common investments because they feature privacy and are also tax deferred. Old-fashioned bank accounts, however, remain the most popular offshore investment based on my clients' port-folios. They seldom produce the best yields but provide less anxiety for those uncomfortable with foreign investing.

Why do so many WealthSaver Trusts invest in foreign mutual funds?

One reason is their investment quality. The fact is that the fastest growth funds are offshore.

U.S. securities and mutual funds are still losing ground. American firms now represent only 26 percent of the world's largest corporations. As recently as 1971, U.S. stock exchanges represented 67 percent of worldwide corporate capitalization. It is now 28 percent. All indicators point to an eroding American investment market. Many foreign stocks now sell at deep-discount prices, with profit/earnings ratios as low as 8. This is half the U.S. P/E ratio of 16. That's only one of many reasons why 70 percent of the world's $10 trillion in equity investments are from foreign sources. We can no longer assume that our U.S. stocks are best. International mutual funds are superb alternatives.

Few Americans realize that they cannot buy foreign funds within the U.S. The IRS discourages international investing by U.S. citizens through addi-tional taxes. This makes foreign funds that much less attractive to U.S. investors than to foreigners. However, the SEC is the chief obstacle to foreign fund sales in the U.S. Investment contracts sold here must first be registered with the Securities and Exchange Commission and also each state where sold. This process is prohibitively expensive. U.S. laws also demand more detailed disclosure than do foreign securities laws. Few offshore mutual funds will invest the time and expense to overcome these restrictive U.S. securities laws.

Foreign funds can be broadly invested or narrowly focused on specific industries. They also can range from the super-conservative to the super-speculative. There is a foreign fund for every taste and pocketbook.

Have offshore mutual funds and securities outperformed similar American Investments?

If you invested *half* your money in foreign stocks over the past 25 years, your portfolio today would be worth about 15 percent more than if you were *fully* invested in American stocks. If you had *fully* invested overseas, you would be 30 percent wealthier. This trend will continue.

Why are annuities the most popular Investments for WealthSaver Trusts?

Annuities are the simplest way to globally invest on a tax-deferred basis. The IRS taxes offshore annuities as it taxes U.S. annuities, *provided* the offshore insurance company that issues the annuities has an option letter from the IRS certifying that the annuity meets U.S. tax-deferred requirements. Tax-deferred annuity investments will obviously grow faster because the tax is payable only when the annuity makes a distribution. And deferred taxes means you do not report the trust income on your U.S. income tax returns *until* there is a distribution to yourself from the annuity.

Swiss annuities also are creditor-protected. While the WealthSaver Trust provides ample protection for its investments, any self-protected investment becomes even more valuable when you encounter serious creditor problems. Finally, foreign insurance companies, particularly the Swiss, are considerably stronger than American insurance companies which are as wobbly as our banks and S&Ls.

I particularly recommend Swiss annuities because they are no-load annuities (no up-front commission) and can be cancelled anytime without penalty or loss of principal. They also are exempt from the 35 percent Swiss withholding tax on interest payments.

Swiss law protects investors against under performance and their interest and dividend income is fully guaranteed by the Swiss government. Investors can also choose between a lump sum payout, rollover into an income annuity, or they can extend the annuity term.

Swiss annuities are purchased by many U.S. tax-sheltered pension plans, Keoughs and IRAs. However, a U.S. trustee must hold the annuity contract, and this greatly reduces its protection from creditors. Several American banks do fulfill that trustee role for a small annual administrative fee.

Can the WealthSaver Trust invest in gold?

American investors often prefer tangible collectibles. Gold is the most popular. Whether gold is your best investment, of course, depends on future gold prices, which is always speculative.

I have several WealthSaver Trust clients whose trusts have invested heavily in the Gold Plan, a unique gold investment program sponsored by the Swiss Uberseebank. If you want gold's investment and privacy qualities without actually buying gold bullion, then you should investigate their Gold Plan.

Gold Plan cost averages, not outguesses, the gold market. Gold Plan allows you to invest a fixed amount each month to buy gold, anticipating a long-term price increase for cost-averaging. Several similar plans are available for securities, but only Gold Plan has this option for precious metals.

Can the WealthSaver Trust own an offshore bank?

A WealthSaver Trust can own its own offshore bank. An offshore bank can be an ideal vehicle through which to more conveniently invest in foreign currency markets, loan money to affiliated entities, reduce or avoid currency controls, arrange for parallel loans and engage in a wide variety of other financial gymnastics. Self-sponsored offshore banking also makes it much easier for affiliated businesses to engage in international trade. For instance, your offshore bank can issue letters of credit to your business or provide third-party guarantees for outside loans. I have established trust-bank combinations for a number of clients with excellent results.

Can the trust funds be held in the U.S. until I have creditor problems?

Many people want their money under their control until it must be relocated. This discomfort is understandable even if unjustified. My own discomfort as an attorney is that the client may not detect approaching danger, and a creditor may peremptorily attach or seize U.S.-based funds. That is one important reason I want my client's money offshore as soon as possible. And the sooner their money is offshore, the sooner they discover the joys of international investing.

WEALTHSAVER HIGHLIGHTS

- To build wealth faster, you must become an international profiteer. There are too many good deals offshore to keep *all* your money in the U.S.

- You cannot limit your investments to only one economy. It's too risky. You must hedge your bets and diversify globally.

- America was once the world's financial citadel, but it is fast losing ground to other countries with far stronger economies. The U.S. dollar symbolizes *less* buying power. You must have more of your funds in foreign currencies if you are to maintain your buying power.

- International investments can be exciting, and there are many to choose from.

- Annuities and mutual funds are the two most popular WealthSaver Trust investments, but even more U.S. wealth is invested in foreign bank accounts.

- You can earn 15 to 25 percent more from your offshore investments than you can from comparable U.S. investments.

- For asset protection and privacy, separate your trust accounts and investments from the United States.

- The WealthSaver Trust is a perfect vehicle for offshore investing. It's your passport to virtually *any* investment in the world and your investments are fully creditor and privacy protected.

5

WEALTHSAVER TAX AND ESTATE PLANNING STRATEGIES

Offshore havens have earned their well-deserved reputation as tax havens because through them you may possibly escape U.S. federal and state taxes through a host of creative offshore financial arrangements. But move cautiously! Many tax schemes are clearly illegal and other are questionable — what I call "gray-zone" tax-saving strategies. Unfortunately, most "safe" offshore tax loopholes have been closed recently by the IRS, and the IRS is enthusiastically seeking to close the few remaining offshore tax advantages. Undoubtedly, the tax professionals will invent new offshore tax opportunities. Offshore tax planning is that never-ending game.

Our goal with the WealthSaver Trust is to achieve legal tax avoidance or tax deferral. Illegal tax evasion is not our objective.

You, however, can take advantage of the WealthSaver Trust to help you legally avoid, defer or reduce income and/or estate taxes. You will also find the WealthSaver Trust a versatile estate-planner to leave your wealth to your loved ones with maximum privacy, efficiency and economy.

To what extent can a WealthSaver Trust save income taxes?

A WealthSaver Trust's ability to save you taxes largely depends upon the WealthSaver Trust.

The most common WealthSaver Trust is the so-called *grantor* trust. This is the standard Offshore Asset Protection Trust used by most Americans. The grantor trust is tax neutral. The trust itself pays no tax as all trust income is taxed directly to the grantor. The grantor trust then is taxed like an S Corporation, a limited partnership or a living trust. It thus offers neither tax advantages nor disadvantages to an American who establishes this trust.

All income to the grantor trust, regardless of type or source, is taxed to the grantor as if the grantor personally earned that income, and notwithstanding whether the grantor is a beneficiary or has a right to any present and future income. No tax is paid by the trust's beneficiaries.

It would thus appear that the opportunity to save income taxes is not a reason to establish a grantor trust, and this is generally true. However, some tax-saving situations are possible when the trust is used in estate planning to reduce estate taxes and in certain other limited instances.

The tax-saving opportunities were far greater prior to the Tax Reform Act of 1976. You could then obtain very direct tax benefits from a WealthSaver Trust. You could, for instance, establish the trust, transfer assets to the trust and avoid U.S. taxes on all income earned by the trust *until* the income was repatriated by the grantor or actually distributed to a U.S. beneficiary.

The IRS now restricts using a grantor WealthSaver Trust for tax deferral the same way it restricts foreign corporations. Section 679 of the U.S. Internal Revenue Code provides that if a U.S. citizen or resident alien transfers property to a foreign trust with another U.S. person as beneficiary, then the grantor that transfers the property must pay U.S. income tax on all income and other gains earned by the trust, *regardless* whether those profits are distributed.

A second trust, the non-grantor trust, is essentially treated as a foreign person for U.S. income tax purposes. As a foreign person, the trust is not ordinarily subject to U.S. income tax on its non-U.S. source income (income earned outside of the United States). There are also U.S. source incomes that the trust could earn without paying U.S. income taxes: interest on bank deposits and certificates of deposit, interest on certain bonds and other loans as well as capital gains from sale of securities. However, the trust, like all foreign persons, is still taxed on the gains from the sale or rental of U.S. real property and dividends from U.S. corporations. Rent, dividends, and most other passive incomes are subject to a U.S. withholding tax of 30 percent of the gross amount, but this can usually be reduced. The non-grantor trust can then accumulate investment earnings tax free if its investments are carefully structured to avoid taxable U.S. income.

The non-grantor trust can *defer* U.S. income taxes *if* you can avoid the grantor trust rules. These rules can only be avoided if either the trust was established by a foreigner who retained no powers that might cause the trust to be considered a grantor trust, or by a U.S. person who since died. Moreover, it can have no U.S. beneficiaries.*The grantor trust is the obvious trust of choice and necessity for most Americans.*

Can the grantor trust save estate and gift taxes?

As a tax-neutral trust, the trust principal of the standard "grantor" WealthSaver Trust is included in the grantor's taxable estate and will not reduce estate taxes.

Transfers to a grantor WealthSaver Trust are ordinarily considered an incomplete gift with no gift tax due upon transfers to the trust. There would be a gift tax if the WealthSaver Trust were considered a foreign trust, or if its beneficiaries accepted a distribution from the trust *prior* to the grantor's death. This does not mean, for instance, that if your children are trust beneficiaries, they can receive nothing from the trust until you die *without* your incurring gift taxes. It is true that your children cannot receive a tax-free *distribution*, but they *can* receive tax-free advances, loans, or income-taxed salaries. There are many ways to transfer trust funds to beneficiaries within your lifetime without the transfer constituting a taxable gift.

How closely does the IRS monitor tax reporting from grantors of WealthSaver Trusts?

The grantor must report the trust income on his tax return in the same way he would report income from a domestic living trust. The difference is that the IRS will not receive informational reports (W-2s, 1099s, K-1s) from the offshore sources (banks, mutual funds) that pay interest, dividends or other income to the trust. The grantor then has a much greater opportunity to evade U.S. income taxes because the IRS has no way to directly learn about taxable income earned by the trust. This essentially puts the grantor of a WealthSaver Trust on the "honor" system.

The IRS is rightfully concerned that it is losing billions of dollars a year in income and estate taxes from Americans with offshore funds. Not all this money, of course, is in WealthSaver Trusts. There are similar opportunities to evade U.S. taxes with offshore companies and bank accounts.

To combat offshore tax evasion, the IRS has proposed legislation (the Tax Compliance Act of 1995) that would, in part, expand the reporting requirements for Americans establishing offshore trusts. Failure to report would subject the grantor and possibly the trustee to severe penalties. Many of these provisions would *not* be retroactive, which is a strong argument for establishing a WealthSaver Trust *before* this law or other new reporting requirements are enacted.

Interestingly, the proposed legislation would force a Cook Island trustee (through his mandatory U.S. agent) to report all trust income where there is a U.S. grantor. This would make the Cook Islands useless to grantors who may be disinclined to report their taxes.

It is uncertain what new tax laws will be enacted to tighten reporting on offshore structures, but two points appear certain: 1) new tax laws are inevitable and 2) there can only be disadvantages when you set up a trust *after* these laws go into effect.

Are there legal ways to use WealthSaver Trusts to avoid U.S. income taxes?

There are several possible ways. Section 679 of the U.S. Internal Revenue Code applies *only* where a U.S. person is a beneficiary of the foreign trust. Thus, Section 679 and its tax consequences to the U.S. grantor may be avoided if no U.S. citizen or resident is a trust beneficiary. For instance, if you have relatives or friends who are foreigners residing outside the U.S., you can establish an offshore trust for *their* benefit without paying U.S. income taxes on the trust's income. Obviously, very few Americans would *not* have at least *some* U.S. beneficiaries.

Even when U.S. persons are beneficiaries, you may still avoid Section 679 by having the prospective beneficiaries form an offshore corporation, with the corporation then named the sole trust beneficiary. An offshore corporation is not considered a U.S. person under Section 679 if at least half its voting power is controlled by non-U.S. persons. Therefore, if your beneficiaries create a foreign corporation with U.S. persons as *minority* shareholders and the foreign beneficiaries as the *majority* shareholders, that foreign corporation as the trust beneficiary would eliminate U.S. taxes on the trust income.

"U.S. person" means any U.S. citizen or resident alien. It also includes a U.S. partnership, U.S. corporation, U.S. estate, or U.S. trust. Foreigners living abroad or foreign corporations that do not do business in the U.S. and are not controlled by U.S. shareholders are not considered U.S. persons.

Do you lose the unified tax credit against assets gifted through the WealthSaver Trust?

You can apply your unified tax credit against assets in the WealthSaver Trust to reduce your taxable estate in the same way you can with a living trust. You can also make gifts from the trust (subject to the same $10,000 per year per donee exemption) to reduce your taxable estate over your lifetime. There are absolutely *no* estate tax disadvantages with the WealthSaver Trust. While the WealthSaver Trust can offer opportunities to reduce or defer estate taxes, it will *not increase* your estate taxes! If you are married you may also prepare spousal WealthSaver Trusts with credit-shelter provisions to maximize the unified tax credit. This, of course, is also a common strategy with spouses with taxable estates who prepare reciprocal "A-B" living trusts.

If the grantor is to pay U.S. taxes on the trust earnings, how does he obtain the funds to pay these taxes?

A WealthSaver Trust ordinarily requires the trustee to pay to the grantor whatever funds are necessary to pay the annual taxes on the trust income. Even absent this trust provision, the trustee can loan the grantor the tax payment if the grantor is also a trust beneficiary. Of course, a grantor may prefer to pay taxes on the trust income from non-trust sources. This is his option, and one commonly exercised.

Wouldn't the WealthSaver Trust also pay taxes in the country where it is established?

WealthSaver Trust havens usually have no taxes or low taxes. Nearly all have a tax below 2 percent. Many havens have double tax treaties with the U.S. that guarantee the trust is not taxed by both the United States *and* the host country. Moreover, taxes abroad can further be avoided by having the IBC that is owned by the trust organized in a no-tax jurisdiction. No trust that I have established pays taxes to any foreign country.

Can the WealthSaver Trust reduce U.S. taxes for American businesses?

A WealthSaver Trust, when structured properly with other offshore companies or structures, may possibly reduce taxable profits for an American business. There are many opportunities and possible arrangements involving controlled and non-controlled foreign corporations, foreign holding companies, foreign sales companies, foreign personal holding companies, passive foreign investment companies and an equal variety of income classifications. You can see the complexities. The point is that it is *possible* to set up foreign companies with your WealthSaver Trust and legally transfer U.S. taxable business income to a *no*-tax offshore company. But this will require detailed planning if it is to legally avoid U.S. taxes. Unless you can save $100,000 or more a year in taxes, it will not be worth the effort.

Many promoters claim they can save taxes for American businesses through wild schemes involving dual trusts connected by intermediary corporations. The problem here is that you *cannot* benefit from diverting U.S. taxable profits to an offshore structure — unless it is a *non*-controlled corporation (NCC). An NCC requires that no *legitimate* foreign partner own less than 50 percent of that foreign company and no American more than 10 percent. Sham partners or nominee foreign stockholders won't work if the IRS can prove you constructively control the offshore company. I have a most extensive analysis of this very tricky situation in a well-outlined free report.

What are the offshore tax-saving opportunities for high-income professionals?

The opportunities here are excellent. One example was the celebrated Nat King Cole's case where Cole set up a Bahamian (WealthSaver) trust to own 100 percent of one corporation that earned U.S. tax-free income from the singer's foreign tours. The same trust owned 50 percent of another corporation that earned U.S. tax-free income on the singer's recordings. Cole, for his labors, was paid a reasonable salary that was taxable. The larger royalty income, however, accumulated tax-free. Through clever structuring of trusts and offshore companies, Nat King Cole legitimately avoided significant U.S. and state income, estate and probate taxes. Tax professionals still use the Nat King Cole case as their blueprint for how a WealthSaver Trust can save taxes for high-income professionals and entertainers who earn some income from outside the U.S.

Cole gave us only one tax-saving formula. But there are other creative tax planners who can appreciate the WealthSaver Trust's versatility.

What are the tax consequences if a foreigner establishes a WealthSaver Trust?

Another *present* way to avoid Section 679 is by establishing a *foreign* grantor trust. A foreign grantor trust is established by a non-U.S. person and qualifies as a grantor trust under the U.S. Internal Revenue Code. A foreign trust can distribute income to American beneficiaries and neither the beneficiary, the foreign trust nor the trust grantor will pay U.S. income tax on the income or distributions. This allows U.S. beneficiaries to legally receive income tax-free. However, the foreign trust *must* be a grantor trust legitimately established by a foreigner.

To qualify as a tax-free foreign grantor trust, the trust's income also must be from foreign sources. To avoid U.S. taxation, the foreign grantor trust also must retain its foreign income. If its foreign income is distributed to U.S. persons as a salary or management fee, for example, it becomes U.S. taxable income.

A foreign grantor trust is recommended if a foreigner desires to leave funds to American relatives or friends. However, if the foreigner establishes the foreign trust under an agreement that allows him to terminate the foreign trust, change beneficiaries or change their respective interests, the trust automatically becomes a grantor trust and subject to U.S. taxes.

If the foreign grantor dies, the foreign trust ceases to have a foreign grantor and all income received by U.S. beneficiaries would then be subject to U.S. tax. This can be avoided by having an offshore corporation, or another foreign entity, act as the grantor. Because these entities have perpetual life, U.S. income taxes can be perpetually avoided.

Congress is presently considering legislation that would treat U.S. beneficiaries as the present owners of their share of a foreign grantor trust. They would then be liable for taxes on that share of the trust's earnings. If enacted, this provision will be retroactive to February 1995, and the foreign grantor trust would then offer no tax benefits over a U.S. grantor trust to American beneficiaries. A potential problem is that an American beneficiary would have a *current* tax liability on *undistributed* income.

This proposed legislation undoubtedly stems from the many "sham" foreign grantor trusts. For example, an American may transfer funds to a foreign business partner, relative or another foreign entity who then becomes the "grantor" of the foreign grantor trust. The IRS will then view the "foreign" grantor as a mere conduit or accommodating transferor and appropriately classify the trust as a U.S. grantor trust for tax purposes.

Is an offshore corporation more effective than a WealthSaver Trust to avoid U.S. income taxes?

Before 1976, Americans who owned a foreign corporation were not taxed on its income until the income was actually received. A foreign corporation not engaged in a U.S. trade or business, or receiving U.S. source income, was *not* subject to U.S. taxes. This, of course, created a strong incentive for Americans to title profit-producing assets and businesses in foreign corporations.

The IRS now taxes undistributed earnings and profits of a controlled foreign corporation (CFC) directly to its United States shareholders. This eliminates potential tax deferrals benefits as the IRS says constructive repatriation of [undistributed] earnings results in an immediate tax to its U.S. shareholder(s).

A controlled foreign corporation is any foreign corporation with U.S. shareholders owning more than 30 percent of the combined voting stock, or more than 50 percent of the total stock, or where any U.S. shareholder (any U.S. citizen, resident alien, trust or other entity) owns 10 percent or more of its voting stock.

The growing popularity of the WealthSaver Trust encouraged arguments that a foreign corporation owned by a grantor trust is not a controlled corporation because the corporation is owned by the trust, not the American grantor of the trust. The IRS nevertheless continues to hold that if the trust is a tax-neutral grantor trust, the corporation the trust owns is *also* American owned and thus taxable as a U.S. corporation. As you can see, the tax savings with an offshore corporation are no better than with a WealthSaver Trust.

What tax returns must the WealthSaver Trust file?

There are several reporting and disclosure requirements involving the formation and administration of a foreign trust. The reporting requirements vary according to the transaction and whether it is a foreign or domestic trust. The following lists the various forms, the transaction or income to be reported and the responsibility for filing.

1. *Form 3520,* Creation of or Transfers to Certain Foreign Trusts. The grantor, transferor, or estate fiduciary (if a testamentary trust) must file this form upon forming a foreign trust with a U.S. beneficiary, or upon the transfer of property or funds to such a trust.

2. *Form 926,* Return by a U.S. Transferor of Property to a Foreign Corporation, Foreign Estate or Trust, or Foreign Partnership. The U.S. transferor files the form.

3. *Form 3520A,* Annual Return of Foreign Trust with U.S. Beneficiaries. If the grantor is treated as the owner of the trust, the grantor must file this annual return if there are any U.S. beneficiaries.

4. *Form 1040*, Schedule B, Part III. A U.S. grantor of a foreign trust must report transfers of assets to the trust. U.S. beneficiaries of a foreign trust also must notify the IRS of their beneficial interest in the foreign trust.

5. *Form 1040NR*. If the foreign trust is not a grantor trust and had U.S. source income, the trustee must file this form to report such income. The trustee also should file *Form 56, Notice Concerning Fiduciary Relationship*.

6. *Form 1041*. If the foreign trust is a grantor trust, in whole or in part, the grantor must file Form 1041 with a statement that shows the trust income taxable to the grantor.

7. *Form 5471*, Information Return of U.S. Persons with Respect to Certain Foreign Corporations. U.S. citizens and residents who are officers, directors or shareholders in certain corporations must file Form 5471.

8. *Form 1078*. This form is for aliens to claim residence in the United States for income tax purposes.

A *domestic* grantor trust — the standard WealthSaver trust — is ordinarily exempt from many of these filings; however, I urge my clients to file with the IRS whenever in doubt. This avoids non-filing penalties if the IRS later determines the trust is a foreign trust rather than a domestic grantor trust. When in doubt *always file with the IRS*. Reporting neither significantly diminishes secrecy nor increases the chances for an audit. Americans with WealthSaver Trusts are not audited more frequently. Accounting fees to prepare these various annual reports are usually under $500. Of course, you should be guided by your professional advisor concerning your filing responsibilities.

How is annuity income taxed when the annuity is owned by a WealthSaver Trust?

Offshore annuities are taxed the same as U.S. annuities. Accumulated income in the annuity is tax-deferred *until* it is paid to the annuitant. The tax liability will then depend on whether distributions are irregular, fixed, installments or payments over a life expectancy.

Irregular distributions are treated as income until *all* deferred income is reported, and thereafter treated as a return on capital. Distributions over a term of years are treated similar to an installment sale. Payments are allocated between ordinary income and return on capital, based on life expectancy.

Most Americans only expect to *defer* taxes offshore. The annuity is their vehicle. The majority of my clients invest through their WealthSaver Trust annuity which allows them to escape U.S. taxes on trust earnings for many years. While a WealthSaver Trust annuity features no particular tax advantages or disadvantages over U.S. annuities, I nevertheless think offshore annuities are a remarkably good way to defer taxes because they will be creditor-protected *and* you can buy many excellent foreign annuities.

How does the private WealthSaver Trust annuity work?

I prepare private annuity contracts for most of my WealthSaver Trusts to provide my client the opportunity to direct his or her own investments, as well as defer taxes. A private annuity operates much like a commercial annuity, except that it is purely a private contract between your trust and yourself, the annuitant, to provide you future income.

Can appreciated assets be transferred to the annuity for purposes of deferring the capital gains tax?

We frequently exchange domestic assets for an annuity from the WealthSaver Trust. For example, you can transfer appreciated land, an apartment house, or shares in your family corporation to the WealthSaver Trust annuity in exchange for the annuity contract. If the annuity later sells the asset, the entire gain is deferred by the annuity until it is distributed. A

WealthSaver Trust private annuity can specifically achieve this tax-deferred exchange if you intend to sell an appreciated U.S. asset.

You can similarly reduce your taxable estate by selling appreciated property to the WealthSaver Trust in exchange for installment payments through a regular installment note, a self-cancelling note (SCIN), a private annuity or a private annuity for a term of years (PATY). Ask your tax advisor which alternative is most desirable for you.

Assets thus sold to the WealthSaver annuity immediately reduce your taxable estate by the value of the assets transferred to the annuity. For instance, if you transfer $250,000 in cash or other assets in exchange for a private annuity with a future payment schedule and died the next day, your taxable estate would be reduced by that same $250,000, and your estate taxes would be reduced about half that amount. You should consider this strategy if you have a taxable estate and wish to leave *your* family more money.

What about estate planning with the WealthSaver Trust? Must you probate WealthSaver Trust assets when the grantor dies?

The WealthSaver Trust allows you to avoid probate the same way you can with the popular living trust.

WealthSaver Trust assets can then be passed to the trust beneficiaries without delay, executor's commission, attorney's fees or other probate expenses. You will need a separate living trust, or a last will, for non-trust assets. While both the WealthSaver Trust and living trust allow you to avoid probate, the WealthSaver Trust generally transfers assets to your heirs with even fewer professional and administrative fees.

Most people transfer only a portion of their assets to their WealthSaver Trust. Other assets are transferred to their domestic living trust because they want to directly control these assets during their lifetime. Rather than use a living trust that offers no asset protection, it is far smarter to title your domestic assets in a limited partnership. The WealthSaver Trust can be the limited partner and own most of the partnership. This combination provides you lifetime control of your assets, excellent asset protection and efficient distribution of your estate upon your death. This is an ideal estate planning arrangement for most families.

The WealthSaver Trust can also become the beneficiary of your living trust or last will, and thus serve as a testamentary trust.

Can the WealthSaver Trust help prevent challenges from a disgruntled heir?

A disgruntled heir cannot easily or successfully challenge the WealthSaver Trust or any distribution the trustee makes from the trust. First, all trust affairs are secretive. Second, the disgruntled heir would be forced to sue in a foreign haven that would be inhospitable to such claims. Third, the WealthSaver Trust, unlike most living trusts, is discretionary. This means the disgruntled heir cannot force a distribution in his or her own favor — regardless of the outcome of any legal challenge. People concerned about challenges from disgruntled heirs will find the WealthSaver Trust their perfect solution.

Can a WealthSaver Trust avoid the forced heirship laws that require minimum bequests to spouses or children?

The WealthSaver Trust is frequently used to avoid the forced heirship laws that compel you to leave a minimum share of your estate to a spouse or children. Several of my clients have established WealthSaver Trusts for precisely that purpose. You must, however, establish your trust in a haven that specifically ignores U.S. forced heirship laws. You also must invest your entire estate in the WealthSaver Trust to avoid claims against domestic assets.

Is the WealthSaver Trust used primarily as a testamentary trust?

The WealthSaver Trust is usually an *inter vivos* trust, or a trust activated during your lifetime. But you can instead fund and activate the WealthSaver Trust only upon your death. The WealthSaver Trust is most commonly administered by the trustee during the grantor's lifetime and also for some period *after* his death. This contrasts to a true testamentary trust that takes effect only upon the grantor's death.

You may want your WealthSaver Trust to continue after your death for the same reasons you would want a domestic testamentary trust: For instance, you have minor children who cannot receive their distribution upon your death. Or you want your wife to have income — but not principal — during her lifetime. Or your spendthrift son cannot be entrusted with the trust assets.

Most WealthSaver Trusts continue after the grantor's death. The conditions for later distribution can be quite elaborately detailed for the trustee through side letters or memorandums of wishes. The WealthSaver Trust can effectively and efficiently serve *any* estate planning purpose and include any provision you would find in any general or special purpose irrevocable testamentary trust.

Isn't the selection of the right trustee even more important when the trustee is to continue the trust after your death?

Selecting the right trustee is *always* important; however, you can ordinarily develop a relationship with your trustee and evaluate his performance and capability to properly administer the trust during your lifetime. If you are dissatisfied you can always replace the trustee through the protector. Confidence in your trustee during your lifetime will give you some assurance that your testamentary trustee will faithfully carry out your wishes *after* you die — a time when your trustee must properly substitute his judgment for yours concerning trust matters. Foreign trust companies and banks are particularly capable of serving as testamentary trustees for even the largest, most complex trusts.

Can the grantor of a WealthSaver Trust later change the beneficiaries or other terms or conditions of distribution?

Absolutely. The grantor can always issue to the trustee a letter of wishes to modify lifetime or testamentary beneficiaries or conditions for distribution. You enjoy nearly the same flexibility with a WealthSaver Trust as you do with a living trust that can always be modified or changed. However, the WealthSaver Trust only gives you the right to *request* these changes. The trustee, in his discretion, ordinarily will honor your new wishes but is *not so obligated*. However, a WealthSaver trustee will not ignore or refuse any reasonable request a grantor may make on so important a point, and the opportunity always exists to replace an uncooperative trustee through the protector.

Charitable trusts have become popular for wealthier Americans. Can charitable bequests from the WealthSaver Trust reduce a taxable estate?

The WealthSaver Trust can be designed to qualify as a charitable remainder trust, charitable remainder unitrust (GRUT), charitable remainder annuity trust (GRAT), or pooled-income fund. These charitable WealthSaver Trusts must be carefully drafted as so-called "purpose" trusts to accomplish both your charitable and asset protection objectives. I have drafted these trusts, and all have been approved by the IRS.

These trusts have become enormously popular with high-wealth individuals in recent years because they allow you to take an immediate deduction for the assets you contribute to the trust while simultaneously insuring yourself a lifetime income from the trust. Your heirs normally receive the value of the donated assets through replacement insurance purchased for a small fraction of the estate tax savings. If your taxable estate is over $3 million, you should consider combining these trusts into a WealthSaver Trust.

Can the WealthSaver Trust also serve as a life insurance trust?

Life insurance trusts are exceptionally important in estate planning. The irrevocable life insurance trust protects the cash value and death benefits under the policy from creditors. Death benefits also are excluded from the taxable estate, unless the grantor dies within three years. To avoid this three-year waiting period, have the WealthSaver Trust buy new insurance. With insurance benefits directly paid to the trust, you avoid probate as well as estate taxes.

Every American with insurance benefits subject to estate taxes should have an irrevocable insurance trust, as should those desiring creditor protection for themselves and their policy beneficiaries. The WealthSaver Trust usually uses its assets to purchase a variable annuity policy on the life of the grantor with the WealthSaver Trust the beneficiary of the policy. Several trust havens allow you to purchase life insurance policies with the premiums segregated from all other funds of the insurer. In effect, a separate fund is created to hold all WealthSaver Trust assets.

Can the WealthSaver Trust give your spouse income during her lifetime and the principal to your children upon her death?

This is a qualified terminable interest property trust (Q-tip trust), a trust most commonly used with a second marriage or non-blended family. Through a side letter or memorandum of wishes, you can request your trustee to distribute the trust assets to coincide with distributions under a Q-tip trust. The wife will then only have a lifetime estate with the remainder interest distributed to the grantor's children or any other named remainder beneficiary. I see quite a few of these arrangements with WealthSaver Trusts, probably because their grantors are concerned that a domestic Q-tip trust would be more easily challenged and overturned. It may also be that the grantor wishes to keep such arrangements more secretive from family members and thus prefers all matters entrusted to a foreign trustee.

Can the WealthSaver Trust shelter assets to qualify for Medicaid coverage for nursing home care?

The WealthSaver Trust can become a so-called Medicaid or catastrophic illness trust. However, it will still be necessary to wait 60 months from the date you transfer assets to the trust before you can qualify for Medicaid. The WealthSaver Trust can also own or protect your home from Medicaid liens. These are liens the government will file against your home to reclaim upon your death what it paid for your care. Your WealthSaver Trust must, of course, be carefully designed for this purpose. My law firm works with several Medicaid and Elder-care attorneys throughout the country to prepare these increasingly important trusts.

Couldn't the WealthSaver Trust tax and estate planning benefits also be obtained with less expensive domestic irrevocable trusts?

The WealthSaver Trust is usually tax-neutral, so it offers few tax advantages over what you could gain through a living trust or limited partnership. And you can accomplish the same estate planning goals through a variety of domestic irrevocable discretionary trusts. However, there are important advantages with the WealthSaver Trust.

First, you can better protect inheritances from legal challenges. You can also avoid the forced heirship laws. The WealthSaver Trust is especially useful for those who want to dispose of their property free of U.S. legal restraints.

The WealthSaver Trust is also an ideal way to segregate and dispose of secretly held assets. This level of privacy cannot be obtained through domestic structures.

More importantly, the WealthSaver Trust gives you immediate asset protection against American creditors. A transfer to a U.S. irrevocable trust, limited partnership or other estate planning structure could expose these assets to a possible fraudulent transfer claim, even many years *after* the transfer.

There are also many more tax advantages than first appear. There are many unique ways to save or defer taxes with the WealthSaver Trust, particularly if your business has global reach and you carefully design your offshore structure.

It is true that the WealthSaver Trust's tax savings and estate planning benefits are not usually primary objectives. Asset protection, privacy and offshore investing are more compelling reasons. Still, no estate planning tool more effectively segregates, titles, protects and distributes your assets with more efficiency, versatility, privacy or safety.

WEALTHSAVER HIGHLIGHTS

- There are several types of WealthSaver Trusts. The most common is the tax-neutral grantor trust.

- The IRS has closed most offshore tax advantages for U.S. businesses; however, through careful planning it is still possible to save or defer taxes. An annuity owned by the WealthSaver Trust is the simplest, most common way to defer taxes.

- Several reports must be filed with the IRS by foreign trusts. Future reporting requirements are expected to become more stringent to prevent tax evasion.

- The WealthSaver Trust greatly reduces legal challenges to bequests. It also allows you to avoid the forced heirship laws. With the WealthSaver Trust, you can leave your wealth as you choose!

- A WealthSaver Trust can be shaped to achieve virtually any estate planning purpose. It's not only as effective as any domestic irrevocable trust but also provides many advantages.

6

A GUIDE TO THE BEST WEALTHSAVER TRUST HAVENS

You must jurisdiction shop from two perspectives: 1) What are your primary goals with your WealthSaver system? and 2) Which havens have the features that will best satisfy those goals?

There is no one "best" haven. Attorneys who specialize in offshore structures each have their "pet" haven. It may be the haven they believe will best protect their client's wealth; however, there also can be serious problems if they do not fully understand the laws of their selected haven, nor how well the haven enforces its laws. Moreover, offshore havens frequently change their laws. Is the selected haven still the best? And did your lawyer consider all the factors before deciding upon the haven? Haven shopping demands a keen understanding of the intricacies of the offshore world.

What is an "offshore haven"?

"Offshore haven" is synonymous with "tax haven," "money haven" or "financial center." Whichever term you use, an "offshore haven" signifies *any* country with a friendlier financial climate than your own. More simply, an offshore haven is anywhere your assets or income enjoy *more* protection and/or privacy and/or *less* taxes. But a financial haven can also make it easier to conduct business, invest, raise capital or exploit your existing capital, often through very creative laws.

How much American money is presently invested offshore?

Nobody really knows because money moves in and out of these financial centers very secretly. Estimates are about $8 trillion is invested internationally. Unquestionably, Americans lead the offshore movement because we have great unrest concerning the safety of our money *and* the unrestricted opportunity to move money offshore. Only four countries are completely free of foreign exchange rules. America is the largest with an estimated $4 trillion invested offshore.

Why are most offshore havens in the Caribbean?

Offshore havens are of every size, variety and political

persuasion and can be found *everywhere*. For instance, Bermuda, the British Virgin Islands and the Bahamas hug America's southeast coast. The Cayman Islands, Turks and Caicos, Nevis and Antigua dot the Caribbean. The Isle of Man and the Channel Islands — Jersey, Guernsey and Sark — shadow England. Switzerland, Liechtenstein, Luxembourg, Hungary and Austria are key European havens. The Philippines, Singapore and Hong Kong serve the Pacific Rim. Cyprus, Malta and Gibraltar are Mediterranean havens.

Money havens cluster in *every* hemisphere, near more industrialized countries with arcane laws that force their wealthier citizens to find friendlier places for their money. But the world is shrinking fast and choice of haven no longer depends on proximity because you can now invest *wherever* your financial objectives are best met. With electronic banking, it is as fast and easy to bank in another hemisphere as next door.

Do offshore havens rise and fall in popularity?

Offshore stars rise and fall very quickly. New, more competitive havens constantly emerge and frequently quite suddenly. Gibraltar, the Cook Islands, Nevis, the Marianas, Belize, Seychelles, Vanuatu, the Turks and Caicos and Montserrat are countries that only in the past few years entered the offshore haven arena.

Because they are newer havens, their laws in many respects are more advantageous and user-friendly, providing them a huge edge over older, less protective havens. Offshore havens seldom attract foreign money by chance. They strategically and creatively restructure their laws to become *more* financially attractive than other havens.

But for every rising star, another loses its glow. For centuries, Switzerland was the bastion of secret banking. However, it is no longer the privacy star. Switzerland's privacy eroded largely due to international (mostly United States) economic and political pressures. The Bahamas and Caymans are also lackluster havens because they are too influenced by the U.S. This prompted the birth of several smaller upstarts, such as the Cook Islands, Gibraltar, Belize, Nevis, and the Turks and Caicos, that guarantee considerably better privacy and protection because they thus far avoided international pressures to compromise the protection they sell. These havens are the rising stars.

Britain spawned the early havens. England is itself a key financial center but is not considered a haven, chiefly because of its many foreign treaties, absence of protective laws and high taxes. But it's very different with the British Commonwealth countries: the Bahamas, the Cayman Islands, British Virgin Islands, Bermuda, Turks and Caicos, Gibraltar and Malta. As independent countries, they each have the political and legal autonomy and enact their own tax, asset protection and banking laws. However, their United Kingdom affiliation gives them economic and political stability.

Whatever the haven's size, history or geography, they all feature laws and banking practices that can in a variety of ways help you to escape taxes or more effectively protect your wealth. While their goals are consistent, they differ markedly in their methods and successes in achieving these goals. The offshore industry has greatly matured since the 1980s. The fastest-growing havens are quite sophisticated — even ingenious — in how they compete for foreign money.

What are the most important features for an offshore haven?

There are many possible factors to consider; however, the five characteristics I consider most important include:

1. Strong asset protection legislation.

2. A predictable legal system.

3. No or low taxes.

4. Laws to protect privacy and confidentiality.

5. No exchange controls.

You, however, must look for those features that can best accomplish your offshore objectives. Those features may be considerably different from the ones here.

What features make a haven good for asset protection?

While a number of havens claim to offer asset protection, I consider only a few adequate for this purpose.

You should consider twelve points when reviewing a haven for asset protection:

1. *Statute of limitations:* The laws must specify a very short time within which any transfers to the trust must be challenged by creditors or be forever barred. Only when you reach this date are you assured that prior transfers to the trust will remain unassailable. The statutes of limitation range from unlimited duration to a brief one year, which, of course, is most favorable.

2. *Non-recognition of foreign judgments:* The haven must not recognize or enforce foreign judgments. At the least, the creditor must be required to re-litigate the case in the haven.

3. *Burden of proof on fraudulent intent:* A creditor who pursues an alleged fraudulent transfer to the trust must be required to prove the transfer

was made with fraudulent intent. The debtor should not be required to prove the opposite.

4. *Standard of proof:* If the creditor must prove fraudulent intent, then the standard of proof should be rigid. Some havens require the creditor to establish fraud by a mere preponderance of the evidence, as is standard in civil cases. Other havens demand that fraud be proven beyond a reasonable doubt, which is the criminal standard and one considerably more difficult to establish.

5. *Ability to freeze assets:* The haven must not allow a creditor to attach or restrain trust assets before judgment.

6. *Invalidity of the trust under a fraudulent transfer:* The haven must protect trust assets that were transferred to the trust before the liability, notwithstanding *subsequent* fraudulent transfers.

7. *Clear differentiation of creditors:* The trust legislation should clearly distinguish between present creditors who can pursue fraudulent conveyances and future creditors who cannot.

8. *Grantor can be a beneficiary*: Some havens do not allow the grantor to be a trust beneficiary.

In others, a grantor-beneficiary forfeits asset protection. The haven should specifically allow the grantor to become a beneficiary, *without* diminishing asset protection.

9. *Grantor can exercise some control:* The trustee (with the concurrence of the protector) must always control the trust; however, the laws should allow the grantor some reasonable authority.

10. *Original laws to apply to immigrant trusts:* An immigrant trust is one relocated to another haven to flee a pursuing creditor who sued in the original haven. The haven laws should then specify whether its laws, or the laws of the new haven shall apply to the immigrant trust.

11. *Conditions precedent to litigation:* The haven should impose procedural obstacles to litigation. For instance, must the creditor post a significant cash bond before litigating? Must the creditor retain counsel from within the haven? Are contingent fees prohibited? These and other procedural restraints can greatly discourage creditor claims against the trust.

12. *Forced heirship override provisions:* Can the grantor exclude a wife or child from inheriting his trust assets? When this is a desired goal,

the haven's laws must specifically override any forced heirship laws of the grantor's state which preclude disinheritance.

Certainly, other factors will influence the asset protection capabilities of a particular haven, and some features can be quite novel. Considering the broad range of possible asset protection features, it is understandable why asset protection lawyers differ in their preferences.

What other considerations or features are important when selecting a haven?

Over 50 features have been identified. Besides those already mentioned, you may also consider:

- Limitations on monetary accumulations.

- Statutes on perpetuities, or a compulsory termination date for the trust.

- Restrictions on corporate trustees.

- Restrictions on protectors.

- Governmental and private fees.

- Allowance of other trusts (such as charitable remainder, insurance, or children's trusts).

- Governmental controls over the trust.

- Recording of trust requirements.

- Grantor residency requirements.

- Registration requirements.

- Trustee residency requirements.

- Protector residency requirements.

- MLAT and other treaties.

- Communications and transportation.

- Banking availability.

- Adequacy of professional services.

How important is the haven's economic and political stability?

Economic and political stability is far less important than the factors mentioned because you generally do not invest within the trust haven. Of course, your haven must have sufficient stability to give you confidence in its laws and enforcement policies. However, if the haven becomes politically or economically unstable, you can then move the trust to a more secure haven. You essentially shop for "laws," not economic climate.

Are the haven's filing and registration fees important?

Costs can be very important. Trust registration costs vary considerably between the havens. Annual filing fees can range from $200 to $2,000 a year. And the fees charged by haven professionals will also vary. You must concern yourself with the annual maintenance costs and only select a low-cost haven that offers you the benefits you want. One reason I prefer Nevis or the Isle of Man is because their maintenance fees are very reasonable. This is not the governing factor in their selection, of course, but since these costs recur each year they must be considered.

How important is good banking, communication and transportation?

It is difficult to find top quality banks in several smaller havens, and you will need a financially sound bank with a good service policy and *no* connection or affiliation with the United States. We frequently select a custodian bank *outside* the haven, which will be inconvenient if the trustee is a resident of the haven. However, banking is not ordinarily a controlling factor in the choice of haven.

Transportation and communication are much less important. Few grantors who establish trusts ever journey to their trust haven — unless the trustee is located there and the grantor frequently meets with the trustee. More often, the trustee is domiciled elsewhere, so the trustee's location then becomes more controlling in terms of convenience.

How serious a factor is the influence of other countries on a haven?

I avoid countries that are too susceptible to another country's economic or political clout, particularly when it is the United States or the United Kingdom. Both of these countries destroyed several existing havens by forced treaties.

Only recently, the United States and United Kingdom signed an enforcement of foreign judgments agreement that renders most U.K. countries useless for asset protection purposes. But to what extent will this treaty influence U.K. Commonwealth nations that we frequently use as havens? This uncertainty diminishes a country's value as a haven.

Most Caribbean havens have already succumbed to U.S. economic pressures and adopted Mutual Legal Assistance Treaties (MLATs) which destroy privacy concerning many economic crimes. A good offshore advisor must sense the potential influence of other countries on the haven.

Which havens are preferred for WealthSaver Trusts?

From over 60 recognized offshore financial centers, 15 have WealthSaver Trust legislation: Angiulla, Bahamas, Barbados, Belize, Bermuda, the Cayman Islands, the Cook Islands, Cyprus, Gibraltar, the Marshall Islands, Mauritius, Nevis, Nieue, Seychelles and the Turks and Caicos Islands. The traditionally popular Isle of Man is now enacting trust legislation after years of allowing common law trusts. Many more havens are expected to enact asset protection (WealthSaver) trust legislation to compete for the enormous international capital in search of protection offshore.

Seven havens are particularly popular for offshore trusts. I discuss them alphabetically because they cannot be ranked. A superior haven for one situation may perform unsatisfactorily in another. The havens unmentioned are not necessarily inferior but may simply be less popular with Americans due to their geography or because they are so new. Some of these havens will undoubtedly become more popular once their advantages become more obvious.

The Bahamas

The Bahamas has 700 islands and 2,000 cays scattered over 100,000 square miles and is located 50 miles from Florida. Its population of 250,000 resides mostly on the island of New Providence and Grand Bahamas. English is the officially spoken language.

Economically, the Bahamas thrive on tourism and its tax-haven industry. Offshore financial activities dominate the islands' products and services: international business companies, insurance companies, banks, personal investment companies, ship registration and trust services.

Bahamian law is based on British common law and is augmented by Bahamian statutes. The supreme court is its highest tribunal over the court of appeals and magistrates court whose jurisdiction is minor civil disputes and criminal offenses. The ultimate court of appeals is the United Kingdom's privy council.

Bahamian banks have freedom from statutory reserve and liquidity requirements. This permits them greater banking flexibility. The Bahamas has no tax treaties to avoid double taxation because it has no direct taxation. Government revenue mainly comes from customs duties and import taxes. The Bahamas also have no personal, corporate, profit, capital gains, estate, death or withholding tax. The Bahamas has strict secrecy and money-laundering laws to discourage crime and to help build a new "anti-crime" reputation. Recent treaties with the U.S. have eroded its once excellent confidentiality.

Bahamian trust law dates back to 1925 but has been frequently amended. Its key features include a two-year statute of limitations for a creditor to pursue a fraudulent conveyance. The creditor must also post a bond equal to 10 percent of the claim and prove a fraudulent conveyance beyond a reasonable doubt.

Belize

Belize, located on the Caribbean seaboard of Central America, has a population of approximately 200,000. Sixty-thousand live in Belize City. English is the official language, although Spanish is also widely spoken. The unit of currency is the Belize dollar with a fixed exchange of BZ $1 to US $1. Telephone, facsimile and telex communications are excellent.

The government has favorable IBC legislation that now attracts more offshore financial activity. Belize law, derived from English common law, is supplemented by local legislation. Its court system compares to the United Kingdom's, and its contract and commercial law is based on English law.

In 1990 the Belize government introduced its own International Business Companies Act, which closely mirrors the IBC laws of the British Virgin Islands and the Bahamas. However, its various amendments aimed at competing with other Caribbean centers give Belize one of the most modern tax-exempt

IBC acts. The IBC legislation permits complete anonymity because members or directors are not required to be filed and, for added protection, allows bearer shares and nominee corporate directors.

Belize trusts are governed by the Belize Trust Act of 1992. It does not recognize foreign judgments, and the trust can be moved to Belize from another jurisdiction. The statute of limitations for a creditor suit is two years. Belize's asset protection laws compare favorably to other asset protection havens; however, it has attracted relatively few WealthSaver Trusts although their numbers are increasing.

The Cayman Islands

The Cayman Islands include three Caribbean islands. The main island, Grand Cayman, is approximately 450 miles south of Florida and its population of approximately 26,000 mostly resides on Grand Cayman. English is the official and spoken language. Its unit of currency is the Cayman Islands dollar.

The Cayman's economy is strong and it enjoys full employment with revenue chiefly derived from financial services and tourism. The Cayman Islands government supports its tax-haven industry as the foundation for its economic growth. The Cayman Islands has its own law courts with appeals to the

Cayman Court of Appeals and ultimately to the United Kingdom's privy council. Cayman Islands law follows English common law.

The Cayman Islands is a British Colony and therefore under the jurisdiction of the United Kingdom. Parliament at Westminster retains the right to legislate. The Cayman Islands is a pure tax haven with no direct taxation levied on its residents or corporations. There are no capital gains, inheritance or gift taxes. No double taxation treaties exist since there are no taxes. The Caymans, however, have signed an exchange of information agreement with the United States.

Cayman trust laws compare closely to those of the Bahamas, which may be explained by the fact that the two jurisdictions pioneered the offshore (WealthSaver) trust. And like the Bahamas, the Caymans' strong anti-crime campaign makes it more difficult to do business there than in most other havens. The chief difficulty with Cayman trust law is its lengthy six-year statute of limitations for creditor claims. More trusts are in the Caymans than elsewhere; however, this is only because it has been in the business longer. Fierce competition from newer, more protective havens and its treaties with the U.S. greatly diminished the Cayman's role as a WealthSaver Trust haven.

Cook Islands

The Cook Islands are 15 islands in the South Pacific Ocean between Tahiti in the east and Samoa and Tonga in the west. Rarotonga is the main island. Half of its population of 19,000 live on Rarotonga. The official language is English although Maori is widely spoken. New Zealand currency is used, and there are certain exchange controls. There are no local restrictions on relocating funds to or from other countries, and funds may be held and business transacted in the Cook Islands in any currency.

The court of the Cook Islands, established in 1964, is the superior court of the islands. Its legal system follows English common law. Appeals are to the Cook Islands Court of Appeal (which must include a current or former judge of the court of appeal of New Zealand) and thereafter to the privy council in England.

The Cook Islands has been considered the premier trust haven since passage of its International Trusts Amendment Acts of 1989 and 1991. Several features that make Cook Island trusts particularly protective include a short two-year statute of limitations from either the date the creditor's claim arose or one year from the date the trust was established. The creditor also must prove the transfer was intended to defraud *that particular creditor.*

The Cook Islands is now one of the most popular trust havens; however, such havens as Nevis now have protective features that many lawyers consider superior to that of the Cook Islands. Moreover, the Cook Islands' trust laws have recently come under attack, particularly from the United States, which raises serious questions about its stability as a future asset protection haven.

Isle of Man

The Isle of Man, located in the Irish Sea close to England, Scotland and Ireland, has a population of approximately 70,000. English is the official and spoken language; however, the island's Celtic origins also produce a unique Gaelic language. Its monetary units are the British pound, Scottish currency and the Isle of Man pound note.

The Isle of Man, with its two traditional sources of income, agriculture and tourism, now emphasizes industrial investment and financial services, which now contribute more than 30 percent to the gross national product. The Isle of Man is the only low-tax financial center in Europe that actively seeks new residents. It has more than 50 licensed banks, including most of the larger international banks. Their financial services are comprehensive, discreet and confidential and compare favorably with banking in Switzerland and Liechtenstein. Besides its good banking are excellent legal, accounting, insurance and other financial services. Isle of Man law is based on English common law, with its civil law legislation chiefly modeled on United Kingdom Acts of Parliament. The island has its own courts. The ultimate court of appeals is the English privy council.

The Isle of Man is a dependency of the British Crown; however, it has never been part of the United Kingdom nor a colony. While the Isle of Man depends upon the United Kingdom for defense and to preside over international affairs, Tynwald remains responsible for all domestic legislation. Apart from a limited treaty with the United Kingdom, the Isle of Man has no double-taxation treaties.

The Isle of Man presently recognizes the WealthSaver Trust by common law, not statute. While its courts have traditionally protected these trusts, the absence of specific trust legislation makes the Isle of Man less desirable than havens with trust legislation since the common law lacks certainty concerning the legal treatment of these trusts. Trust legislation is now under enactment and it is expected to make the Isle of Man an even more popular WealthSaver Trust havens.

Nevis

Nevis is located in the Leeward Islands approximately 1,200 miles southeast of Miami. The current population is 8,000 and 35,000 reside in the neighboring island of St. Kitts. English is its official and commercial language. Its official unit of currency is the Eastern Caribbean dollar. There are no currency exchange controls. Nevis offers excellent communications, including direct dialing to the U.S., Canada and Europe, as well as worldwide telex, facsimile and telegraph services. Direct airline service is available to most major cities.

Nevis offers an attractive package for offshore investors. No taxes are levied on income, dividends or other distributions from a Nevis company which are foreign-sourced. There is no filing of corporate financial returns, annual reports, or changes of shareholders, directors or officers. Shareholders, directors and officers may be of any nationality and reside anywhere. The secretary may be a corporate entity or an individual, and companies may serve as directors. The 1983 constitution provides for a federal parliament headed officially by the governor-general. The Nevis cabinet is headed by the premier as leader of the majority party in the house of assembly. Its legal system is based upon English common law and is served by a high court of justice and a court of appeal. Nevis was a British colony from 1628 until 1983 when it became independent and joined the federation of St. Kitts-Nevis, which remains an active member of the British Commonwealth. Nevis is a democracy based upon the British parliamentary system and has an elected local assembly.

The Nevis trust ordinances govern its WealthSaver Trusts. Nevis has perhaps the strongest trust laws, even surpassing perhaps those of the Cook Islands. Nevis, for instance, requires creditors to file a claim within one year from the date the trust was established. The creditor must also file a $25,000 litigation bond and prove a fraudulent conveyance beyond a reasonable doubt. Nevis is rapidly becoming the haven of choice for WealthSaver Trusts.

Turks and Caicos

The Turks and Caicos, north of Haiti and the Dominican Republic, sit at the base of the Bahama Islands. Its population is 9,500, and English is the official language. The unit of currency is the U.S. dollar. Communications are excellent.

The Turks and Caicos enjoy an escalating foreign investment industry. However, pending new legislation, the Turks and Caicos is closed to all branches or subsidiaries of many international banks.

The legal system is based on English common law. The Turks and Caicos are a self-governing British Crown colony.

WealthSaver Trusts on the Turks and Caicos Islands are governed by the Trust Ordinance of 1990. There are no exceptional features to the islands' trust laws, which offer only average protection. Nevertheless, the Turks and Caicos attracts a disproportionately large share of trusts, which more reflects its great ability to market its modest financial advantages.

Which of these havens is best for a WealthSaver Trust?

You can't select *one* haven because you need at least *three* havens.

First, you must choose the haven for the WealthSaver Trust. A trust haven *must* provide exceptionally solid asset protection and privacy laws. As I stated, from about 15 possible havens, only seven are commonly used by Americans. Their protective differences may be so subtle that offshore trust specialists disagree on which is best.

The WealthSaver Trusts I established are mostly in Nevis. I consider its extremely short statute of limitation for creditor claims an enormous selling point. However, I have established WealthSaver Trusts in several other popular havens, including the Isle of Man, Turks and Caicos and the Bahamas. Several of my colleagues prefer Belize; others, the Bahamas or the Cook Islands. We each have our favorites because we each attach different values to their legal characteristics and features.

Nor is today's "best" haven necessarily tomorrow' "best." Trust havens are fiercely competitive and continuously revamp their laws to gain a competitive advantage. Moreover, new asset protection havens constantly emerge as we have seen with Gibraltar, Belize, Nieue, and the Seychelles. You must continuously shop for your best deal.

Selecting a trust haven is only the first step. You must also select the haven for the trust-owned International Business Corporation (IBC). This haven must feature good incorporation or company laws and privacy, no or low taxes and most of the other general attributes you would demand from a trust haven. But you primarily want good company laws. At the minimum it must allow non-resident nominee directors, bearer shares and low administrative costs. While you can organize your IBC in a number of havens, I prefer the Bahamas or British Virgin Islands, primarily because of their excellent company laws and low organizational costs. Other popular company havens are the Isle of Man, Belize, Panama, the Cayman Islands,

Costa Rica, Turks and Caicos, Seychelles and Montserrat.

Finally, you must select your investment havens. Those are the countries where you can invest profitably and safely. Many countries do not tax foreign investors, while providing reasonable secrecy, good economic and political stability, no exchange controls and sound investments. The United States , United Kingdom or Canada is not an option when you have creditors.

Your professional advisors usually select the haven, but they must first clearly understand your financial and legal objectives if they are to intelligently match you to *your* best haven. Your advisors must also patiently invest the time and effort to fully understand your needs.

What features make an attractive International Business Corporation (IBC) haven?

To enhance privacy, you should choose a haven different from the trust haven. Moreover, the best trust havens are seldom the best for the IBC. Good IBC havens have company laws that feature:

- Nominative or bearer shares.

- Sole directorships.

- Corporate entities allowed as officers or directors.

- Minimal capital requirements.

- No recording of officer or director changes.

- Minimal registration fees.

- No taxes on income earned outside the haven.

- No required annual stockholder or director meetings.

- No required annual financial statements.

- Complete privacy and confidentiality.

The most popular IBC havens are the British Virgin Islands (BVI), the Bahamas and Seychelles. Nieue, the Caymans, Belize and Panama are also popular. The Isle of Man, Guernsey and Jersey are also used regularly, particularly by U.K. residents.

What features are most important with investment havens?

Aside from the investment opportunities that the country may offer, you would also want an economically and politically stable jurisdiction. The haven must either be tax-free for foreign investors or have tax treaties with the U.S. or home country that prevent double-taxation. Privacy is also a factor, although the account would not be established in the grantor's name. We also want the country to offer reasonable asset protection and have few ties to the United States.

For instance, the Isle of Man or the Channel Islands present the same investment opportunities as the United Kingdom, but with considerably greater privacy and protection.

For investment purposes, I usually recommend Switzerland, Liechtenstein, Luxembourg, Austria, Hungary, the Isle of Man, the Channel Islands or one of the British Commonwealth havens — usually the Bahamas or Cayman Islands. Of course, there are other suitable countries for investing.

What is the most common mistake when selecting an offshore haven?

There are *two* common mistakes. First, many American lawyers and their clients become victimized by the aggressive marketing campaigns from these various havens. These havens are fiercely competitive and their promotional materials can convincingly portray illusive advantages. You must look deeper into their laws and practices.

Again, you must know what features are most important to you and whether these features actually exist in the haven or arise from advertising puffery. The features you counted on *must* be there when you need them! You cannot take this for granted. As a post-doctoral research scholar at the London School of Economics, I researched how trust havens perform in practice. This study convinced me that promises and practice can be very different. What these havens *say* they will do, and what they actually do, are frequently very different.

The second mistake is the propensity for lawyers to use the same haven for every client. That, of course, is no more sensible than choosing the same house or car for every client. But offshore lawyers often do just that because it is *their* easiest path. These lawyers become familiar and comfortable with one haven and its professional infrastructure, and their trust practice can then become "cookie-cutters" affairs. These lawyers ignore that the haven that is right for one client is not necessarily the best for another.

WEALTHSAVER HIGHLIGHTS

- From over 60 offshore havens, only a handful are suitable for WealthSaver Trusts.

- You cannot select your WealthSaver Trust haven *until* you decide the features that are most valuable to you.

- Selecting the right haven for the IBC is no less

important than choosing the right trust haven. Your trust haven needs good *trust* laws. Your IBC haven needs good *company* laws.

- Your professional advisor must be familiar with every possible haven and *match* you to *your* right haven.

- WealthSaver Trust havens constantly update their laws. And new havens appear. The increasingly competitive offshore industry constantly produces countries to help you better preserve your wealth.

7

ON THE ROAD TO FINANCIAL FREEDOM

Having read this far, you may agree that the WealthSaver Trust can give you the financial freedom it has provided so many other Americans. But there are still so many questions: How much does it cost to establish or maintain? Who can guide me professionally? What are my potential pitfalls — and how do I avoid them? How do I intelligently start? Should I start? How can I be sure a WealthSaver Trust is for me?

There are answers to these questions, but to insure that they are the correct answers requires you to seriously consider your needs and your goals. That is the key to a sound financial future. And as every successful individual knows — every worthwhile journey begins with that all-important and most difficult first step! It can be your step toward a financial freedom you never thought possible. Without that step you have only read another book

Dr. Goldstein, having come this far with you, how can I decide whether the WealthSaver Trust is right for me?

The WealthSaver Trust, for all its benefits, is not for everyone. You must be realistic about what the WealthSaver Trust can do for you. And what it can accomplish may not be enough to justify the cost or effort involved in establishing the trust.

To decide whether the trust can adequately benefit you may require a candid discussion with the right professional. No book can replace a professional evaluation of your own situation. And you may easily misinterpret or incorrectly apply general information to your situation from a book such as this.

I will say that you are *not* a good candidate for a WealthSaver Trust if you cannot become comfortable with your money beyond your control and in the hands of a foreign trustee. I receive several calls daily from people who are otherwise perfect candidates for a WealthSaver Trust but cannot bear to part with their money. This, of course, is understandable.

Many of these people will eventually overcome their fears. They often have no choice if they wish to protect their wealth. Slowly, even super-cautiously, they will take the plunge. Others never overcome their uneasiness. Nothing can coax them to send their money offshore. You also may be uncomfortable with your wealth offshore. You cannot force the issue. You must decide whether it is only a matter of learning more about the WealthSaver Trust or a case of chronic insecurity over such arrangements. Even when the WealthSaver Trust is vital to your security, you may refuse its strong protection and instead accept less protective domestic asset protection strategies. That, of course, is almost always a mistake. You cannot compromise when it comes to asset protection. You need the best protection possible — if your wealth is important to you.

How can I become comfortable with the WealthSaver Trust concept?

Educate yourself! Start by reading everything you can on the subject. There are several good books and journals I recommend concerning offshore havens and WealthSaver (asset protection) Trusts. I particularly recommend:

- *Offshore Investment Journal*
  10 Camptown Road
  Irvington NJ 07111

- *Offshore Financial Review*
  Greystoke Place
  London ENGLAND EC4A1ND

- *Financial Times*
  FT Publications
  14 E 60th St
  New York NY 10022

- *Tax Haven Reporter*
  Box SS6781
  Nassau BAHAMAS

- *Trusts and Trustees*
  The Mill Office
  Wendens Ambo
  Saffron Walden
  Essex CB11 4JX
  UNITED KINGDOM

Garrett Publishing has a number of excellent books on asset protection, privacy and offshore finance. Request our most recent catalog by writing us at Garrett Publishing, 384 South Military Trail, Deerfield Beach, Florida, 33442, or phoning (954) 480-8543.

Also write: Scope Books Ltd, 62 Murray Rd, Horudean, Hants 90895L, UNITED KINGDOM

If there is one book to read, what else could it possibly be but my very own *Offshore Havens?* This best-seller reveals how the offshore world *really* works.

You can obtain your copy at most bookstores or order directly from Garrett Publishing. (See Appendix.)

Insecurity, of course, is born from unfamiliarity. Many of my clients balk at my suggestion of a WealthSaver Trust until they read a few books and articles on the topic from a variety of other sources. Perhaps after six months of independent investigation they conclude that their fears were ungrounded and the potential benefits are indeed very real. They can then proceed with more confidence, but only then!

Are there other ways to reduce concerns about transferring control of your wealth?

Talk to people! Many more Americans have WealthSaver Trusts than you might expect. Your professional advisors can probably put you in touch with a few. Or call me for names. I have many clients who will candidly talk to you about their WealthSaver Trust experience.

Almost every one of these people has asked the very same questions or experienced your same concerns about the WealthSaver Trust. How safe will my money be? Will the trustee run away with my money or lose it on some crazy investment? Can I *really* get my money back if I need it? These undoubtedly reflect a few of your concerns.

That's why you should talk to a few individuals who once expressed your same thoughts. You will not only find them quite satisfied, but you will also find their money safe and secure. I know my clients are quite pleased with *their* WealthSaver Trusts because I consistently hear comments such as this from one satisfied client: "You never realize how vulnerable your wealth is here in the U.S. — until it is safely sheltered in a WealthSaver Trust." Or this comment from a Los Angeles physician: "Before I was nervous about putting my money offshore. Now I get nervous thinking how easily I could have lost it here."

Knowledge *is* the key to confidence, and confidence, the key to action. That's why I will enthusiastically spend many hours answering every question a client may ask about the WealthSaver Trust. It's essential because *only* knowledge can give my clients the confidence that they need to proceed. Their WealthSaver Trust program invariably gets under way with more enthusiasm and functions more smoothly because their fears are calmed. These informed people no longer see the venture as a journey on uncharted waters. They know what to expect. Their questions are answered. Their concerns are resolved. And that again is why I wrote this book. I want people who *can* benefit from a WealthSaver Trust to know about this remarkable financial tool.

You may find the *very best* way to overcome your concerns is to start slow. Invest only a few dollars in your WealthSaver Trust, and invest more only as your confidence grows — as it will.

How do you locate and select the right professional advisors to establish your WealthSaver Trust?

Knowing about the WealthSaver Trust cannot substitute for good professional advice. Your education can only help you to more *intelligently* select your advisors and to work with them more effectively.

Selecting your legal advisor can be hazardous. While most offshore professionals are honest, trustworthy and knowledgeable, every business has its crooks and incompetents. My profession is no exception.

You must start with an attorney who is well-experienced with offshore trusts. Never "buy" your trust from a non-lawyer or a so-called trust company that sells offshore companies or trusts. Most of these firms are reputable, but many others are frauds who sell worthless trusts to an unsuspecting public. Another problem with acquiring a trust from a commercial firm is that your communications with that firm are not privileged as they would be with an attorney. Confidentiality is important.

Still another reason for an attorney to handle your trust is that you will want to coordinate your WealthSaver Trust with your domestic asset protection and estate planning. This, of course, is more difficult to achieve when you do not have appropriate professional representation on your offshore matters.

A lawyer's license, of course, hardly insures competence, but it at least implies an individual sufficiently honest to stay licensed. However, an inexperienced lawyer is inadequate at best and dangerous at worst. A WealthSaver Trust involves complex legal, financial, and tax issues. The most conscientious attorney can know very little about the technical aspects of a WealthSaver Trust unless he is well experienced with them *and* stays abreast of the rapidly changing rules concerning these trusts.

Do check your attorney's references but also respect confidentiality and never pry into his or her client's financial affairs. Also check whether your prospective lawyer is a member of the Offshore Institute. The more active offshore specialists usually belong to this worldwide organization whose members must display exceptionally high professional standards and offshore experience. The Oxford Club is another popular organization for offshore lawyers.

Where do you find an experienced offshore attorney? Start with the two organizations I mentioned.

The bar associations do not yet maintain rosters of off-shore lawyers; however, your regular attorney may find you one by inquiring within legal circles. Can I assist you? I maintain offices in several major cities and have formed WealthSaver Trusts for clients in virtually *every* state. I also work closely with attorneys who refer WealthSaver Trust clients to me, as well as with accountants, financial planners and other professionals who require a trust for their clients.

What specific legal services will be required?

Your attorney's primary responsibility is to prepare the trust and form the subsidiary International Business Corporation or other affiliated structures. Your lawyer may also prepare a private annuity contract and the many other ancillary documents. Together with your trustee, your lawyer will then handle or oversee the transfer of assets to the trust and file all necessary governmental reports. Your attorney may also recommend prospective trustees, protectors, investment advisors, accountants and the other professionals who will organize and administer the trust.

I believe that education is your lawyer's most important function. It is the most important service I perform for *my* clients when establishing a trust. I spend whatever time is necessary to thoroughly answer their every question about the WealthSaver Trust. Oftentimes I walk through nearly all the questions I answer here. But without these answers, the client will be unnecessarily concerned or have false expectations about the trust or make serious mistakes in dealing with the trust. Forming the WealthSaver Trust is not the time-consuming task. The time a client requires to fully understand it is where the hours are spent. If *your* attorney lacks the time, patience or knowledge to answer your every question or concern about the WealthSaver Trust, then you must find one who does.

What steps are necessary to implement a WealthSaver Trust?

The steps in implementing a WealthSaver Trust are considerably more complex than meets the eye. It can take a month or two and involve frequent client conferences, extensive correspondence with the foreign advisors, preparation of numerous documents, investigation of unique problems or issues and overseeing the transfer of assets while generally making certain that everything is coordinated and proceeding accordingly.

I generally start with a thorough review of my client's affairs and the reasons for establishing a trust. This will include a review of any present or possible claims. From this information we can select the appropriate haven and begin to recruit prospective trustees and other foreign professionals to administer the trust.

The second step is to design the offshore structure. The trust will usually be combined with one or two IBCs, limited liability companies or limited partnerships. The proper organizational structure involves many complex issues, particularly taxation. During this second phase I will also identify and draft special provisions or features for the trust that can add protection or privacy for my client.

The third step toward implementation is to actually draft the numerous documents to create an operational WealthSaver Trust. These documents contain relatively standard provisions, but there can also be considerable customization of the trust, particularly in areas of estate planning.

Step four is to select the foreign professionals for the trust and to coordinate matters between them. This frequently requires considerable redrafting of documents to accommodate their special requirements and concerns.

Step five is to assist in transferring the various assets to the trust and to file required tax forms.

Of course, these steps do not occur in true sequence. They can overlap with considerable backtracking and review.

The most important phase is the period *after* the trust is established to monitor whether:

- the parties are complying with all the legal, tax and reporting requirements;

- The parties have their activities well-organized and working relationships are functioning smoothly;

- The trust and its investments continue to be in appropriate havens;

- The offshore trust is coordinated with the domestic financial plans, to best meet the client's asset protection, tax, investment and estate planning.

We review at least annually whether the trust is still properly organized to accommodate the client's personal situation.

About how much will it cost to set up a complete WealthSaver Trust?

Certain law firms charge as much as $35,000 for a customized offshore trust. On the low end are the commercial offshore firms who provide boiler-plate asset protection trusts for under $7,000. About $10,000 to $15,000 is the fee range a qualified attorney will charge to form a complete WealthSaver Trust, including the IBC, an annuity contract and all ancillary legal matters. Filing fees as well as trustee, protector or investment advisory fees are billed separately. Fees, of course, will vary based upon the anticipated size of the trust, the trust haven, special problems or concerns, complexities in tax and estate planning and special client needs or accommodations.

The "bargain-priced" trusts from several offshore companies will be the most expensive if they prove worthless and you have no recourse. Offshore firms frequently tout low-priced trusts as loss leaders so they can become your overpriced trustee, or to push overpriced annuities or other questionable financial products to the unsuspecting. Always hire an experienced lawyer who is accountable, qualified, conflict-free and can serve you faithfully and competently. You must expect to pay a fair fee to receive the quality service that you need. You must consider the costs to establish a WealthSaver Trust as an insurance premium. It certainly is the most cost-effective insurance available when you consider that it is a one-time expense and can protect unlimited wealth against virtually any claim over your entire lifetime.

What are the annual fees and costs to maintain a WealthSaver Trust?

That is a very important question because the annual maintenance fees can mount over the years. Ongoing annual fees usually include the trustee and protector fees, as well as annual filing fees for the trust and IBC. There will also be modest accounting fees for the annual reports.

Offshore trustees charge about $2,000 a year, with a range between $1,000 and $4,000. Some trustees will also charge an initial engagement fee of about $1,000. Trustee fees will also depend upon the trust size and its activities. A trustee may surcharge a trust over $3 million or one with excessive investment trades. You must always obtain a schedule of itemized charges *before* you engage the trustee. And do not be afraid to negotiate.

Professional protectors charge about half the trustee's fee. However, a friend, relative or business associate may serve as your protector to avoid this expense. Annual accounting fees average about $500. Filing fees depend upon the selected haven but will average about $700 annually.

You should budget about $2,500 toward annual administrative costs. This also should not be considered an expense but an excellent investment because your money can earn considerably more offshore and easily cover these nominal costs.

Can you discontinue the trust or must these administrative fees continue each year?

Because the trust is irrevocable, you cannot usually revoke or terminate it. However your protector and trustee may together have the power to revoke the trust. But you can borrow or distribute all the trust funds and leave an empty trust. You can also then dismiss your foreign trustee and assume the trusteeship of your trust by incorporating your own trust company in the jurisdiction where your trust is registered. Your cost will then be only a few hundred dollars a year for filing fees. Or you can choose to disqualify the trust by withholding the necessary filing fees. You therefore commit yourself to no future expenses beyond that which you consider necessary to protect yourself.

How do I find and select a good trustee?

There are many excellent trustees to serve all the offshore havens. They are mostly lawyers or chartered accountants who must pass rigid examinations to qualify for trusteeships.

Your trustee should administer at least 50 trusts. Only an active trustee can provide you the widest array of services. The trustees who serve my clients must also be fully bonded by an A-rated insurance company for the full value of their portfolios.

While qualifications are important you and your trustee must also be comfortable with each other. You must test your relationship. Discuss your objectives, investment preferences and financial philosophies. Anticipate any special considerations that you will require, such as whether you will need loans from the trust. This is one relationship that you cannot accept on faith alone. Your trustee must be cooperative, flexible and responsive to your needs. But mostly, your trustee must be someone you can get along with. That's why I encourage my clients to personally meet with several prospective trustees so they can then intelligently compare and choose the most appropriate trustee.

As with your lawyer and other professionals, you must also check your trustee's references. How many clients do they serve? How satisfied are their clients? How has their firm grown? Who else within the firm may handle your account? Will you be assigned only one individual to handle your account? Will they provide client references? Bank references? Proof of bonding? Can they deliver the services you need — such as portfolio management? Are they accessible? Responsive?

Location is important for convenience purposes. You may not meet personally with your trustee, but a trustee in a time zone 12 hours behind your own will limit you to nocturnal communications.

Also choose the right size and type of trustee firm. If you are more conservative, or have a larger portfolio, you may prefer a bank trustee. Many old-line banks, such as Barclay's, Royal Bank of Scotland and Westminster Bank, have active trust departments. You may feel more secure with a major institutional trustee; however, non-institutional trustees have an excellent record and are quite safe. A bank will charge higher trustee fees than will a private trust company. And banks are less flexible. I use bank trustees only with the most cautious clients. My other clients have been quite satisfied with their non-institutional trustees.

Trustees within a haven are competitive and therefore charge competitive fees. However, you should compare fees and not hesitate to negotiate a lower fee — provided it will not compromise the quality of service that you receive.

The Offshore Institute includes as members a number of professional foreign trustees. The several offshore journals also advertise trusteeship services. Your attorney may have several trustees to recommend to you, and, of course, I would be pleased to refer you to several trustees who have well-served my clients.

What factors are most important when selecting a protector?

You must remember the protector's role: to veto

trustee actions and, if necessary, replace the trustee. This should not make the trustee and protector adversaries, and, in fact, they *must* work cooperatively.

A good protector only needs common sense and a basic understanding of finance and how things work in the offshore environment. Most importantly, the protector must have the time and willingness to oversee the trustee and approve his actions. Your best candidate may be a friend, business associate or close relative. As the grantor, you should neither be the trust protector nor choose someone you obviously control.

You can retain professional protectors who frequently are from the same firms that as act as trustees. For obvious reasons, you must never select a protector recommended by your trustee. In most cases, your attorney will locate your professional protector.

An American protector is acceptable, provided the trust is not under creditor pursuit. When that occurs, a foreign protector should be substituted to insulate the protector from U.S. legal service or the compulsory disclosure of the trust's affairs.

How do you coordinate the WealthSaver Trust's financial activities?

You will probably continue to keep at least part of your wealth within the United States. You must then integrate your offshore finances with your domestic financial arrangements.

First, you should involve your financial advisors *before* investing offshore. You and your advisor must coordinate many important issues, including how to reduce income and estate taxes, pass your offshore and domestic assets to your heirs, blend investments, and control and repatriate your offshore funds. Your WealthSaver Trust only becomes one important part of your financial jigsaw puzzle, and it must fit perfectly.

A properly structured and coordinated WealthSaver Trust will enhance financial planning in many ways, producing higher-yield investments, lower taxes, more creative estate plans, privacy and asset protection. The WealthSaver Trust can be the best foundation for superior financial planning.

What is the biggest mistake people make when establishing their WealthSaver Trust?

They lack clear objectives about what they want the trust to do. Only with clear objectives can you successfully customize the trust to your needs. Only when you know what you most want the trust to accomplish can you select your *right* haven and the *right* trust provisions to achieve those goals. Remember the old expression, "To get there you must first know where you want to go." So it is with the WealthSaver Trust.

You may well discover that you can as effectively accomplish your objectives without a

WealthSaver Trust. Or that the trust's cost and required effort is not worth its marginal benefits.

What is certain is that without achievable objectives your trust will fail. You are almost certain to choose the wrong haven, the wrong offshore organizational structure or the wrong professionals to administer your trust.

You will need specific strategies to achieve your objectives and specific tactics to achieve those strategies. So we return to objectives. Consider them most carefully. You may, for instance, establish your WealthSaver Trust for one specific reason and fail to consider the many other possible benefits it can provide you. The lawsuit defendant who seeks asset protection may find he can both protect his assets *and* save taxes. Or you may only seek offshore investment opportunities while overlooking asset protection and privacy. WealthSaver Trusts offer many benefits. You must always look beyond your one big reason for creating the WealthSaver Trust and exploit *every* WealthSaver opportunity that awaits you.

What is the most costly mistake?

You want financial security and freedom but will *not* do what is necessary to achieve it.

For every five people who will read this book, four will enthusiastically agree that the WealthSaver

Trust would greatly benefit them. Three will endlessly procrastinate. Or remain fearful or skeptical. Or be blocked by the expense. Or never find the time. Only one of the five will proceed and find financial security with a WealthSaver Trust.

You cannot afford delay if you truly want financial freedom. You cannot afford excuses. You cannot afford to wait until tomorrow because *tomorrow:*

- you can get sued.

- you can have the IRS chasing you.

- you can get divorced.

- can bring creditors and bankruptcy.

- the government may confiscate your assets.

- our U.S. economy can crash and destroy your wealth.

- Uncle Sam may freeze your money.

- you can lose your wealth in so many ways that are unimaginable... *today!*

So make yourself this pledge. If the WealthSaver Trust still makes sense to you *after* you have reviewed your situation with an experienced advisor, then don't wait any longer. Why delay the many powerful financial benefits *that can be yours* when financial freedom is only a phone call away!

WEALTHSAVER HIGHLIGHTS

- The WealthSaver Trust is not for everybody. You must clearly understand what it can and cannot do for you.

- If you have anxiety about losing control over your money, you must then learn more about offshore finance. It is the one best way to reduce your fears and build confidence.

- A WealthSaver Trust requires experienced, qualified professional advisors. You cannot trust your financial future to amateurs.

- The WealthSaver Trust doesn't cost. It is your best investment to protect and conserve your wealth.

- Have your financial advisors properly coordinate your WealthSaver Trust activities with your domestic financial planning.

- Only when you fully understand your offshore financial objectives can you achieve them.

- Why procrastinate? Let the WealthSaver Trust take you down that all-important road to lifelong financial freedom!

Offshore Havens

A whole new world for wealth protection!

Arnold S. Goldstein, Ph.D.

Helps investors deal with the complexities of offshore financial privacy and international profiteering. As making money within the shores of the United States becomes more cumbersome, foreign investments are expected to grow tremendously. *Offshore Havens* introduces the reader to the dynamic world of international investments and the potential profits found abroad. Among other topics, readers discover:

- The ins and outs of foreign money havens.
- Legal ways to avoid taxes and protect assets using offshore havens.
- The best offshore money havens, and why they're so good.
- How to gain privacy and avoid the pitfalls of offshore banking.
- The benefits of conducting your business offshore.

Stock No.: OH 700
$29.95 6" x 9"
256 pages Hard cover
ISBN 1-880539-27-6

The Family Limited Partnership Book

Arnold S. Goldstein, Ph.D

Family limited partnerships have become America's hottest financial planning tool. They're the ideal way to protect assets and save income and state taxes while preserving full control of your wealth. Here's the book that teaches how to develop a comprehensive plan to protect your family's assets. Includes easy-to-complete documents to create a family limited partnership, as well as chapters on:

• The benefits of the family limited partnership.
• How to use the family limited partnership for asset protection.
• How to achieve tax savings with the family limited partnership.
• The family limited partnership as an estate planning tool.

Stock No.: FLPB 104
$24.95 8.5" x 11"
256 pages Soft cover
ISBN 1-880539-39-X